MW01245926

The Successful Writing Group

The Successful Writing Group

Embrace a Mentor

H. Dean Fisher

Seventh Battle Publishing

Hardcover edition ISBN-13: 978-1-952811-19-7
Kindle ebook edition ISBN-13: 978-1-952811-18-0

Author photo by: John Kilker - JohnJKilker.com
Cover image: artist proksima, licensed through iStock

Printed in the United States of America

First hardcover printing: June, 2023
First ebook printing: June, 2023
The Successful Writing Group: Embrace a Mentor
Seventh Battle Publishing
Nicholson, PA

CONTENTS

AUTHOR'S NOTES   vii

Introduction   1

1   Thou Shalt Not Kill   5

2   Writing Groups   16

3   The Mentors   25

4   The Passive Freeloaders   37

5   The Active Freeloaders   48

6   Location, Location, Location...   82

7   It's All About the Program   94

Conclusion   103

ABOUT THE AUTHOR   105
BOOKS BY H. DEAN FISHER   107

H. Dean Classics 2: "The Successful Writing Group: Embrace a Mentor (20th Anniversary Edition)"

This book was born from a conversation in a bar more than 20 years ago. I met an independent publisher, and we were chatting about the pros and cons of writing groups, especially the people who attend them. Most writing group members are there to help and contribute, but there are some people who do real harm to others, knowingly or unknowingly, especially when they make cutting, personal remarks.

We chatted about the need for a book that would look at writing groups through a critical lens, that would analyze the group dynamics, and that would make recommendations for improving toxic groups. He loved the idea of a book like this, and I agreed to write it.

However, I had just started work toward an MA in Journalism, and I couldn't devote as much time to writing as I planned. By the time it was complete, the publisher had shifted focus and was no longer interested in a book like this. Then my MA turned into a PhD, I started a new job, moved across the country, and had a child – and suddenly this manuscript was 20 years old.

The content, however, is still incredibly relevant to writing groups I interact with today. Modes of communication have changed (texts instead of emails, and the meeting apps instead of posters on a wall), but the basics of writers gathering together to improve their stories has not changed at all. Group dynamics 20 years ago are pretty much the same as they are today. The Mentors who help grow writers are still as compassionately lifting their fellows now as they were then.

I updated the content to reflect what I've learned since I first wrote this book, especially new interactions with people online and other formats for hosting meetings. It's been several years since I led my last writing group, but my time doing the work is some of the best of my entire life. I had the privilege of knowing some exceptional Mentors, and I'm thrilled that so many of them remain lifelong friends.

Special thank you to so many people, but most especially to the Write Right Critique Group of Lubbock, TX, and all the great friends who saw this manuscript in its earliest forms. Our time together was special. Thank you to all those who helped instill in me a love of writing groups, including KJ (it's been far too long...), Larry

AUTHOR'S NOTES

Abdallah, James Stoddard, Kristyn Kingston Rose, Ann Lavendar, Everett Kergosien, Jeremy Hoffpauir, and Kim Hunt Harris.

Introduction

ANCIENT HISTORY

Flash back to 1979. I'm 9 years old, and I've just completed my first novel. I am proud of this masterpiece. Thirty-two pages long, including pictures, a gripping plot only loosely based on "Star Wars," a hero who always does the right thing, aliens who need a good thrashing, and a galaxy that needs saving. (No, there was no princess in my masterpiece. All that romantic stuff was just too weird for my 9-year-old brain.)

I told my mother to get the envelope ready – this book was headed for Universal Studios, and I was headed for international fame before I was 10. She said she wanted to read it first.

Not a problem! Of course, my own mother can read this phenomenal book before everyone else in the world proclaims my brilliance. After all, she's my mother. She deserves those kinds of perks from her creatively brilliant, soon-to-be financially independent, 9-year-old son.

Fifteen minutes later, she returned my masterpiece and said she had some "suggestions" to make it better. Hey, a tweaked metaphor here, a stronger verb there – I had no problem with any of that.

We sat on the living room floor, and my mother critiqued my masterpiece page-by-page: First of all, novels didn't generally consist of stick-figure drawings. If I wanted to write a comic book, we should work on my artistic ability. Second, what was my hero's motivation? He was flying around the galaxy for no reason when he suddenly ran into hostile aliens? It needed something stronger – a bigger punch. Next, I called my first novel "The Seventh Battle," but there was only one big battle in the entire novel. What was the point of the title? Did it relate to something before the book started? Were there supposed to be six battles before this one? If so, I should probably share that information with the reader.

And on we went...to page two. <sigh>

That kind of unhelpful criticism continued for what felt like another 1,849 hours before my mother finally released me to bed for the night. I tossed my shredded manuscript into the corner and vowed never to let my mother read one of my stories again. She obviously didn't have the refined taste of my target audience, those legions of "Star Wars" fans who would adore my story. I moped around the house for a week, mulling over why my own mother couldn't recognize brilliance when she read it...and then I started on the book's sequel.

It was also called "The Seventh Battle."

MODERN HISTORY

Flash forward to 1992, and I had just graduated college. Call it Providence if you like, but it was more likely that I couldn't stop talking about my writing. I told a complete stranger that I had just finished a short story (I'm sure it must have related to our conversation somehow), and she told me about a writing group she attended. I was intrigued. A group of people who did nothing but read their writing to each other and suggest improvements to the stories? What a great idea.

I printed out my latest masterpiece and went to the meeting fully prepared to wow them with my creative genius. I read my short story to them, and they applauded like the devoted fans I knew they would be. Then they asked me questions.

My character was just wandering around at the beginning of the story, but...why? What was his purpose? Where was he going? What were his motivations before the story opened? It might need something more, maybe something with a bigger punch to it. Something to really hook the reader.

Second, what was my hero's motivation? Why was he going from point A to point B? Did he have a purpose to his quest? If so, I should share it with my readers so they could be along for all the emotions my hero experienced.

Next, what was the point of the title? What did it mean? Couldn't I have come up with a stronger title, something that gave a clearer idea of where the story was going? Or something to better intrigue my audience?

I went home, threw my shredded manuscript into the corner, and moped for the next week because those people obviously couldn't see my brilliance.

When I next sat down at my computer to write, I thought about what the members of that critique group had said. Maybe my protagonist's motivation was a little weak, and that title could be punched up a bit. I fiddled and tweaked, and I cut and paste – but most of all, I tried to look at my story through the eyes of those people who knew nothing about me or my writing. Not only did I realize they might be right, but I also realized that my mother might have known what she was talking about 13 years earlier. That was a scary thought.

WHY I DON'T LET A "FREELOADER" READ MY WORK

Since that first meeting in 1992, I have been a member of four writing groups across the country: one in Minnesota, two in North Dakota, and one in Texas. I started one group in North Dakota, and I led the Texas group for nearly a decade, both face-to-face and online. I have met published novelists, prize-winning poets, self-published writers, inspirational authors, playwrights, authors with books optioned by Hollywood...and the list goes on. I have worked with writers from ages 14 to 92. I have witnessed stories move from simple ideas bounced around the writing table to completed manuscripts to published stories – many times with some of my own suggestions included.

On the flip side, however, I have met writers who simply didn't want to work. Either the writing was "perfect" before I saw it, or the writer knew I could never understand the "depth" of his work, or the writer simply did not want to change the words on the page. Why mess with obvious perfection?

Notice I said the "writer" did not want to change. I'm sure you've heard the cliché, the one that says writing is 10 percent work and 90 percent rework. A "writer" is someone willing to do that first 10 percent. The writer will sit at the computer and create worlds, characters, plot lines, and themes all day – and know they're perfect the moment those elements burst into existence. An author, however, goes to the next step and does the rework. The author is never satisfied with that first 10 percent, that initial burst of inspiration. The author writes the words and then points a critical eye back at those words. Could that have been better written? Did that metaphor fly? Was it a cliché? What about that character? Plot point? Dialogue? Anyone can do that first 10 percent – anyone can write. It takes someone dedicated to the craft who is willing to truly author something.

My mother recognized I had more work to do when I wrote "The Seventh Battle." That first writing group recognized I had more work to do when I wrote that short story. It wasn't until I agreed to do that work – and I was finally willing to look seriously at their suggestions – that I became an author in the true sense of a writer working to master his craft.

The trick, however, is to find a reader who will give you the criticism you need – not the praise you desire. I wanted my mother to tell me I was a genius. I wanted that writing group to tell me I was the best writer they'd ever read.

My mother told me my book needed work. The writing group told me to get back to my computer and revise.

Did it hurt? Absolutely. Did I want to hear it? Absolutely not.

Did I become a better writer because of it? Yes.

But you can't let a Freeloader read your work. You have to let a Mentor read your work. A Mentor is a person with an eye toward good writing, well-crafted sentences. It's somebody who's not afraid to tell you the story is bad – and then offer suggestions to raise it up. A Freeloader says, "This is great." A Mentor says, "You can do better." That's why I don't let Freeloaders read my work.

Even if I didn't recognize it then, my mother is a Mentor. Even if I didn't want to see it in 1992, that first writing group was full of Mentors. When I was in college, I met the best Mentor I've ever known – and I married her.

I'll tell you how you can use Mentors to improve your writing.

1

Thou Shalt Not Kill

The Problem

The primary rule of every writing group must be: "Do not kill."

And don't try to tell me you don't know what can kill a writer; you know exactly what would harm you the most. They're the critiques that are aimed at the heart, not the paper. The comments that tell the writer that not only does the story need improvement, but that the writer obviously never took a single English class in his life. In fact, if he'd known even the basics of writing, he would have known that stories are NEVER written that way. Well, people may have written like that at some point in history, but I'm sure that ancient civilizations crumbled because of the bad quality of writing they produced.

Writing to kill is writing comments like:

"Oh, please! Like that would ever happen."

"Writing today needs to be excellent. Yours is not."

"I can't believe you wrote this trash."

Ever heard those remarks? The first two were aimed at me, and the third was received by a friend – a published author with multiple books on the shelf. Those are examples of some of the worst that can be done by a writing Freeloader. (I'll talk more about writing Freeloaders in chapters 3 and 4.)

It may seem silly to someone who's never written a story in his life, but most authors say their stories are their babies. When someone comes along and says "this is trash," it's the equivalent of telling a parent that his child is going to Hell in a handbasket. (Forget the fact that most people today couldn't even define "handbasket.") It not only hurts, but it rips into an author's heart. When an author sees those words scribbled across his manuscript, he also sees the blood seeping from between the pages. The light of exhilaration he felt when he first breathed life into that batch of words suddenly dims in the realization that someone else thought those words were trash. It seems like something we should already know, but we either forget or we don't know it yet: Words can kill.

This is a point I'll allude to throughout the book. Nothing can kill a budding author faster than another budding author cutting him down – in other words, writing to kill.

Several years ago I sent three of my works to a contest, one novel and two short stories. The procedure was straightforward: People involved with the conference (other writing group members, local authors, local writing instructors, etc.) conducted the preliminary judging, and the best of the preliminaries moved on to the final round of judging conducted by editors and agents from New York.

I was informed that one of my manuscripts had placed, and the prizes would be distributed at the awards luncheon during the weekend conference. Of course, I attended. (I recommend you attend conferences every chance you get. They're an excellent way to network, receive feedback on your writing, and ask those burning questions that your friends never seem able to answer.) At the conference, I was awarded first place for my novel "The Jungle God" (recently celebrating its 20th-anniversary publication just a couple years ago). I was ecstatic! Even better, however, the New York editor who conducted the final judging took me aside to personally praise my work.

When I looked at the critiques I received from the preliminary judges, however, the comments were less than flattering. My novel, which took first place and received such high praise from the New York editor, got mediocre comments at best from the preliminary judges. I was told that my manuscript was weak, that my characters were cardboard, that the language I'd invented for my alien race was confusing and unnecessary, and that I didn't know how to write a synopsis.

My short stories fared even worse. The preliminary judges' comments were harsh, telling me that I didn't know how to construct a story, that I didn't know how to write believable characters, and that my characters' religious views were simply wrong.

While some of those comments may have had merit, the tone in which they were given to me did not. There's a difference between telling an author that his characters need more fleshing out and scribbling across the page, "You expect me to believe this?" or "Oh, please! Like that would ever happen!"

As to the criticism of my characters' religious beliefs, while the moral of a story certainly affects that story's reception, it has little place in the evaluation of how well a story is written. One of my favorite authors, Orson Scott Card, is quite vocal about his religious beliefs, and I don't agree with several of them. However, I've ordered his books months in advance because he's an incredible author who weaves wonderfully complex stories with vivid characters. If your definition of quality writing must correspond with your definition of religion, then you're going to cut down your list of potentially readable authors by at least half.

When I pointed a more critical eye at those stories, however, I saw that I had several passive verbs, my characters needed to be more fully rounded to sustain themselves through the course of the stories, and the alien language I created was more complex than it needed to be. All legitimate criticisms of my work. As for the moral of my story that so offended one judge's religious beliefs, it was obvious from the specific comments the judge wrote in the margins that he had missed the story's point regarding religious institutions. A fault of the judge? Hardly. If the moral of my story is so convoluted that it can be misinterpreted as saying the exact opposite of what I intended, then I, the author, failed to communicate my point. I needed to work on every problem those judges pointed out to me.

However, as valid as some of the critiques may have been, the comments the judges used to convey those critiques were not. In fact, the written remarks on my short stories were so brutal that if I'd not also heard that New York editor's praise, I might never have written another story again. (Although my wife would have sat me down at the computer and made me write if I'd told her I was quitting. She's a great motivator that way.)

I'm not alone in those kinds of examples, either. I've spoken with other authors who have received harsh criticism, not only from contests, but also from agents, editors, and other writing group members. We'd like to make excuses for the critics – he was having a bad day, his spouse had just left him, a meteor had fallen on his car. There's no way to know what's going on in another person's life, especially regarding the agents and editors who likely live thousands of miles away. The most likely reason for agents and editors being harsh is that they live in offices piled high with manuscripts from authors who believe they're the next Hemmingway, King, or Steele – and they're not. It's easy to imagine that an editor, after reading his 1,582nd misspelled word in one day, might be a little snippy. There's not much I can say about instances like that except to buck up, take a good, distanced look at your manuscript, and see if the essence of the comments is valid. Did you really misspell the word "the"? Then fix it.

Writing group members are a different problem, though. We might see them a couple times a month. We may count them as our friends. We hope they're sympathetic with our plight as struggling writers. When those people write comments that cut deep – "take an English class and learn to write!" – it hurts. And it can kill a budding career long before that career comes close to sprouting.

This point is important enough that I wanted to spend this first chapter discussing nothing but "Thou shalt not kill." Preach it. Practice it. Do not tolerate it when someone else breaks this rule.

Are you tempted to write those kinds of comments? Don't.

The Solution

It's easy to say "thou shalt not." It's much harder to live it. When the first thought that comes to your mind is, "take an English class!", it's easy to let that also be the first thing you write. When the characters in the story are nothing more than cardboard cutouts; when the author recently discovered alliteration – and uses it everywhere; when you've read the first six pages and realized it was still the introductory paragraph; when you've re-read that sentence 28 times, but you have no idea what the author wrote...it's tempting to let your frustration show with every biting comment scribbled illegibly across the page.

Resist temptation.

There are better, more productive ways to write those comments, ways that will build up the author, that will help her figure out how to write better instead of chastising her for not yet knowing something. Remember, there was a time when you didn't know how to do that either. You had to learn. Now it's time to help someone else learn. It's time to be a Mentor.

Let's start with one basic assumption and go from there. This is something I believe wholeheartedly when I teach my university classes and when I work with aspiring authors: Every person who attends a writing group for any period of time can and will learn to become a better writer and editor. Some people may learn more slowly than others, but everyone will learn. There is something about being in the company of other writers for an extended period of time that brings out the best in a writer. She'll take more time in her writing. She'll work harder on her rewrites. She'll edit more thoroughly. Those traits – maybe fostered simply to avoid the embarrassment of being told she misspelled another word – will work their way into the author's daily practice until better prose comes naturally. Voila! Better writing.

There are, of course, a couple exceptions to this basic assumption. First, a writer may not attend the writing group long enough to become a better writer. For whatever reason – too little time, moving out of town, personalities don't click, or she's too proud to accept any critique of her manuscript – this writer leaves before any of the lessons from the group really sink in. That happens, and there's nothing that can be done about it.

Second, the writer may be improving, but the group can't see it because the writer already finished the book. She spent the past five years working on this manuscript, and she knows it has problems. She's working on a new novel, but she doesn't want to bring that one to be critiqued until the first one's critiqued from start to finish. So, she spends two years bringing one chapter at a time to each meeting, and you spend two years telling her that she's misspelled "the" every time she wrote it.

And third, some writers just don't want to improve. I'll talk about this more in chapter four, but there are writers – for a variety of reasons – who see no reason to change. Remember what I said about myself at 9 years old? My mother had very real critiques of my writing, but I wasn't ready to hear those critiques. My writing was "perfect." The only reason I wasn't a best-selling millionaire was that Universal Studios hadn't seen the manuscript – and that's part of the problem with those "perfect" writers, that they haven't even grown up enough to know that Universal Studios doesn't publish novels.

There's little you can do about writers who fall into the first category, the ones who don't stay around long enough to learn. You hope they find another writing group, and you go on with your life.

Patience is the best trait with writers in the second category, the ones who want that entire first novel critiqued before they show you anything new. Keep correcting that writer, but look forward to that new book whenever she brings it. It will be better.

As for the writers who are already perfect and don't want to hear your critiques, it's been my experience they don't attend writing groups for very long, especially after you point out that the writing is not perfect. That's a comment an immature writer never wants to hear.

Now that we've established our basic assumption – that every writer who attends a writing group can and will become a better writer – let's work on how to critique that writer so she can grow.

Your goal as an editor should be to help that writer reach the next level in her writing. If all writing is placed on a scale of 1-5, with one being the worst and five being the best, and she's writing at level 2 right now, then you want to help her reach level 3. Once she's at level 3, then push her to achieve level 4. Even people you think are at level 5 can still improve. I've read people I believed were level 5 authors, but I've still found misplaced commas and weak verbs in their writing. That happens because we're all human. We all get tired when we write; we all have off days when we just don't feel like writing or editing. Those things are natural, and they let mistakes slip into our writing. It's our job as editors to work those mistakes and weaknesses out of the writing, and we need to find ways to encourage the authors never to make those mistakes again – in essence, to bump up their writing to the next level.

The "five levels of writing" idea is a good place to start this discussion of moving to the next level. Here are my personal definitions of the five levels of writing:

LEVEL	POSITIVE TRAITS	NEGATIVE TRAITS
1)	Typed, not handwritten	Unintended caricatures
		Rambling, pointless sentences
		Writing full of clichés
2)	Few clichés	Passive verbs
	Few rambling sentences	Bad formatting
		No descriptions
		Story begins too early AND ends too late
		Story is bland and predictable
		Flat characters
		Run-on sentences
3)	Better verbs, but...	...verbs weak
	Manuscript formatted, but...	...much of the format is wrong
	Better characters, but...	...characters weak
	Better sentences, but...	...sentences weak
	Some descriptive words, but...	...description weak
	Interesting story, but...	...predictable story
4)	Good characters	
	Direct sentences, but...	...sentences not vibrant
		Story begins too early OR ends too late
5)	Strong verbs	
	Good format, ready for submission	
	Vibrant, living characters	
	Evocative sentences	
	Powerful descriptions	
	Story begins and ends at the right places	
	Story keeps the reader guessing and turning pages	

Table 1: Fisher's 5 Levels of Writing

If those descriptions seem ambiguous, that's because writing is more of an art than a science. Some may think that perfect, level-5 writing contains no errors in grammar, spelling, or punctuation, but that definition also describes a dictionary. While I've met some people who read dictionaries in their spare time, no one has ever accused a dictionary of containing a gripping plot. On the other hand, the most interesting story in the world could be rendered indecipherable with enough grammar, spelling, and punctuation errors. Good writing is about hitting the right mix of excellent English with an engaging narrative.

As the editor, you need to decide what part of the author's story needs the most work. I tend to focus on the English rules for lower-level writers and the narrative structure for upper-level writers. For example, if the author misspells that nefarious "the" 23 times in the first paragraph, then I start at that point with my critique. Characterization and plot will take care of themselves over time (or we can deal with them later), but if the author is having trouble with grammar, spelling, and punctuation, she won't get past the first reader at most publishing houses. When she gets the English rules flowing well, then I start thinking more seriously about the narrative elements, the characters and plot. That's the system I use, and you'll come up with your own set of criteria for evaluating writing as you edit more stories.

The important thing to remember, though, is that you point the writer in the direction of better writing. You won't accomplish that with biting comments like "take an English class!"

But what do you say to that writer who misspells "the" every other time she writes it? The first couple times she does it, it's easy to write the correct spelling in the margin and read on. By the tenth time, it's become distracting, and you're getting aggravated. But by the time you get to page 92 and she hasn't spelled "the" correctly yet, you're probably far beyond aggravated – likely on your way to throwing the manuscript down the garbage disposal. It's times like that when it might feel really good to scribble in blood-red ink across the entire length of the page, "Take an English class already!" That is the time when you most need to back away from the manuscript, set your emotions aside, and put your focus firmly back on the writing. Go back to the first page and write, "You misspelled 'the' throughout the manuscript. Use 'Find & Replace' to correct it." You're done. You've pointed out the problem, and you've informed the author how to fix it.

Those two points are exactly the approach you need to take with every critical comment you make on an author's manuscript:

1) Point out the problem.

2) Offer an alternative that corrects the problem.

As an example, let's look back at what I call Level 3 writing. Among other things, the manuscript contains: Passive verbs, flat characters, and run-on sentences. Passive verbs slow down the writing, flat characters make it hard to care about the story, and run-on sentences just confuse the reader.

The passive-verb sentence reads: "The gun was shot." That "was" must go. It's vague, lifeless, and slows down the story.

A mean-spirited, harsh editor would write something like: "So????", "Why should I care???", or "This is BORRRRRING!" While these comments may make the editor feel better, they do nothing for the author. They don't tell the author what the problem is, and they certainly don't give her any ideas for fixing it.

Instead, you – the editor – should write something like, "'Was' is a passive verb. Rewrite to make it more active." You've followed the bare-bones minimum of the two-step process I listed above. You pointed out the problem ("'Was' is a passive verb"), and you offered an alternative ("Rewrite to make it more active").

You should also consider that the author may not know what you're talking about when you say "passive verb." I was a junior in college before anyone to the time to define passive verbs for me. The entire concept of a verb being "active" or "passive" confused me. I was still confused seven years later when a college professor attended my writing group and circled every "was," "were," and "to be" verb in my entire story. Then he did the second part of our two-step process – he offered alternatives to fix the problem.

So after writing "Make it more active" on the manuscript, take a few more seconds and give the author an example (or two) of what you mean. It doesn't have to be a 20-page treatise on the merits of active verbs; a simple, two-step example will work fine. Like this:

"You wrote: 'The gun was shot'

"Try: 'He shot the gun.'

"Or: 'He pulled the trigger.'"

You point out the problem, and you offer an alternative. If the author is confused about the concept of passive verbs, you can take some time during the group meeting to discuss it with her. You'll probably find that she's not the only confused member of your group. Everyone else will be thrilled to have this discussion because they know active verbs will improve their own writing – but they're not in the hot seat of a critique, so they can sit back comfortably and soak it all in.

Now look back at the two approaches to editing: the harsh, critical approach and the friendly, helpful approach. The harsh editor says, "Learn to write!" She makes a personal attack, she offers nothing constructive, and – worst of all – she flaunts her disdain for her fellow writer. That critique screams to the rest of the group, "I'm part of an elite group of writers who KNOW how to write. Bow before my genius." Critiques like that can crush the spirit of new writers.

However, the friendly, helpful critique accomplishes a few good things for the writer. First, it points out exactly what the problem is. She won't scratch her head and think, "Well...what's wrong with it?" You've told her.

Second, the friendly critique helps her grow as an author. It's one thing to simply point out the problem – even the harsh editor can sometimes accomplish that. It's quite another, however, to share your knowledge and help another writer step up to the next level – to be a Mentor.

And third, the friendly critique shows your fellow writer that you care she grows into the fine author she can truly become. It's an odd fact of editing, but just as the mean-spirited critique tells the author you don't care two bits about her, the friendly critique tells her that you're someone who will help. You're a friend to her writing.

This same process will work for the other things I mentioned, the flat characters and run-on sentences. Tell the author what she's doing wrong, and tell her how to fix it. That two-step process will help your friends – the members of your writing group – step up to the next level in their writing.

2

Writing Groups

What they are and how they work

So, what is a writing group?

At the most basic level, it's a group of people who get together to improve each other's writing. That's it. There's nothing mystical or secret about a writing group.

Hidden within that basic definition, however, you'll find endless variety. Some groups read stories aloud; others read silently. Sometimes the author reads the story, and sometimes the group has a designated reader who reads every story aloud. Some groups get together and critique everything at the meeting then and there. Other groups distribute stories, take them home, and discuss their critiques at the following meeting.

Groups meet at all times of the day, evening, or night. They meet once a month, twice a month, every week, and sometimes even a couple times a week.

Groups exist for specific genres. Other groups accept writers of any genre. Sometimes groups focus on only fiction, non-fiction, or poetry.

People hold meetings at libraries, community centers, bookstores, homes, parks...anywhere they can find the room, the time, and fellow writers.

Writing groups can also be confused with "book groups," but they are not the same. While book group members and writing group members can (and often do) attend each other's meetings, the purpose of the two groups is distinctly different. You may already be a member of a book group and know what I'm talking about. In fact, some of my writing group descriptions may sound familiar to you if you attend any book groups.

Primarily, book groups and writing groups differ in their goals. A book group seeks to make better readers; a writing group seeks to make better writers. As such, book group members will read published work (sometimes fiction, sometimes non-fiction) and discuss what the author said and what the characters did. Writing group members will read unpublished work and discuss what the author could have said or what the characters could have done – with the goal of making the final, published piece that much better.

Finding a group

Finding a writing group that meets your needs can feel impossible. For the most part, writers are solitary people who don't like to stand out in a crowd or boast about their chosen profession. Many writers are doing great if they'll just hand out a business card. But advertise? Blatantly promote themselves to the outside world? Stand up and boldly proclaim, "I am a writer" to anyone who will listen? Nope!

In fact, no Hollywood stereotype comes as close to the mark as its portrayal of writers. You have the loner in the woods writing his book in "The Secret Window," the writer who never has any excitement except when she pretends to be characters in her own books in "Romancing the Stone" and "The Lost City," and the writer sinking into writer's-block oblivion in "Funny Farm." My favorite film about writers, "Throw Momma from the Train," shows the extreme end of advice-giving and -taking when a writer decides to live out Hitchcock's murder-swapping "Strangers on a Train" scenario with his self-obsessed, creative-writing instructor.

I don't know of any writer friends who have tangled with a Colombian drug lord or tried to pitch an 80-year-old woman from a moving train, but all the writer eccentricities are wonderfully portrayed in those films: the hours alone, staring at a blank screen or piece of paper; the talk-to-yourself brainstorming sessions; the obsession with keeping your idea to yourself because you know every other writer wants to steal it; the constant fight to avoid distractions.

While most writers don't display every quirk those movies portray, almost every writer shuns the spotlight. When he's at a party and the talk turns to his writing, he glances away, shuffles his feet, and answers noncommittally. If he's brave enough to actually jump into the conversation, he sheepishly mentions, "Yeah, I write." But if he's employed anywhere else for any amount of time and making any other money from that second employer, he'll always clarify "But, it's not my day-job." Face it: Publicity is not a writer's strong point.

That one little trait, however, makes it extremely difficult to find a writing group. The same bug that keeps that writer from promoting himself doesn't even let the thought enter his mind that he might want to promote the writing group he attends. I've lived in several cities throughout my life, and it's always a chore trying to find a local writing group. In Bismarck, North Dakota, I didn't know any groups existed until I started one of my own – and then someone told me there was another group in town. In Lubbock, Texas, I spent months asking if anyone knew of a writing group. Not even my coworkers at Barnes & Noble had heard of a writing group in town – until the day my manager announced to the store that the local writing group was hosting a coffee social. That group had existed for 50 years, but no one I asked had heard of them.

All of this can lead a writer to wonder if there is any hope of finding a writing group in his own town. The answer is yes, but you must be more patient than I was in Bismarck. Keep looking. Keep asking.

While the local bookstores are a great place to start, the chain stores may not always give you the best answers. I worked at Barnes & Noble, and my wife worked at Waldenbooks (remember them?). Those stores had so much going on each month and had so many employees on staff that there was no way everyone working there knew everything going on within their own store – and certainly not elsewhere within the city. Whatever you do, don't ask the first employee you find in the aisles. Ask to speak with the manager or the community relations director if the store employs one.

Even better, however, would be to contact independent bookstores. They tend to be smaller stores with fewer employees, and it's easier for them to disseminate information to everyone. The average employee is more likely to know if the store hosts a group or if one exists around town.

You should also contact the libraries, newspapers, and radio stations in your area. Again, don't be satisfied with asking the first person who answers the phone or the first guy you meet behind the reception counter. Ask to speak with someone in the know, such as the man in charge of community announcements, or an around-town editor, or the person who books the library's community rooms. You can also contact a high school or college English department or your city parks & recreation department.

Use your online resources. Google is your friend; use the MeetUp app; check all of the social media announcement pages, the city's community page, the library's online events calendar, etc. The point is, as difficult as these shy writers make it for you to find them, they are out there. Keep looking; don't give up.

How writing groups work: The rules

Most writing groups are structured around one person who is in charge. It's possible to operate a writing group by committee, but I've never tried. That central person could be an often-published author, a devoted writer, the most organized person attending the group, or simply the only one willing to be in charge. I've seen (and been) several kinds of leaders. It usually doesn't matter why that person's in charge, as long as she gets the job done.

All writing groups have a set of rules, written or unwritten – but I recommend written rules. I've already told you my primary rule, "Thou shalt not kill." Another rule I use is to never critique with a red pen. A red pen makes a story look as if it's either been edited by that grumpy, fourth grade teacher who hated children, or like someone stabbed your story 38,000 times and the pages bled across the table. Neither of those images appeals to me, so I insist that my members use some other color instead of red. I prefer blue. The blue pen doesn't convey any hack-n-slash images, and the color shows up well enough that the writer can see my marks.

I also set a rule regarding the number of pages that can be distributed by an author at each meeting. That rule becomes much more important as more people attend the group. If there are four people at each meeting, and the group meets once a month, then it's not a big deal if everyone passes out 30 (maybe even 50) pages. I can read and edit a couple hundred pages in a month. However, when a group reaches 15 members and meets every two weeks, you have to lay down the law: no more than 10 pages at a time from anyone. Double-spaced. Yes, some writing group members – and I won't name names, but his initials are HDF – may try to get around that rule by single-spacing the pages. Be diligent about enforcing the page limits and the double-spacing.

How writing groups work: Special speakers

As odd as it sounds, some writing groups emphasize the writing much less than other groups. This is another case where writing groups are not created equally. While one group pushes its members to produce new articles and stories to hand out at every meeting (sometimes even assigning story ideas to recalcitrant writers), other groups don't care if a writer ever produces new work and may even consider it an interruption to the agenda if a writer tries to distribute a story for critique. I'll display my personal bias and tell you that I don't care for that kind of writing group. Having said that, let me be as fair and unbiased as I can and tell you how groups like that operate. A writing group that does not distribute and critique writers' work usually operates with a classroom format. The meeting facilitator arranges a special speaker (possibly herself; possibly an area writer) to speak to the group about a writing topic. It could be feature writing, magazine submissions, character development, plotting, or any number of other special topics. Those kinds of meetings are usually informative, sometimes memorable, and oftentimes lead a writer to believe she's accomplishing something even when she hasn't written a single word.

Seriously, though, I have conducted meetings such as that, and as long as the facilitator puts extra effort into arranging a speaker who has something useful to share, those kinds of meetings can be inspiring and informative. Too often, though, the special speaker becomes the inspiration for the unproductive writer. Such an unproductive writer comes to a meeting, hears a speaker, and says, "That was great! I can do that!" If the writer is highly motivated, she may go home and actually put fingers to keyboard – especially if she knows her group is expecting a chapter from her in two weeks. However, if she knows that the next meeting will have a different special speaker talking about some other topic, then the pressure is off to actually produce content. She may write that chapter tomorrow, or maybe next week, next month, or...well, whenever she gets to it within the next couple decades. In the meantime, she's attending those great meetings where special speakers line up to tell her what a wonderful writer she could be.

Special speakers work best when they are truly special. Special in the sense that they have something important to share; special because their writing displays a certain technique your writer friends need to learn; but most of all, special because those kinds of special speakers don't speak to the group on a regular basis. The event is special; the speaker is special; the topic is special. Put the emphasis on "special," and those kinds of speakers are fine. Make "special" the norm, however, and you're serving a recipe for writer atrophy.

When that special speaker shows up, there are a few things you want her to accomplish. First, she should not be there simply to promote her latest book. Some promotion can be tolerated – in fact, a certain amount of promotion is usually implied by the invitation to speak, especially if she's a recently published author who's excited about her new book. However, she should have something useful to share with your fellow writers, some tidbit of writing wisdom they couldn't get anywhere else. It might be her plotting technique, the way she creates vibrant characters, or her flair for description. Maybe she has a talent for writing perfect query letters, or she's worked with one agent for 20 years and is willing to share the secret of a long relationship. Whatever your reason for inviting her, she should stick to the script with as few commercial breaks as possible.

Second, she should give your members plenty of opportunities to ask questions. A well-rehearsed speech is wonderful for the body of her presentation, but at some point she must be willing to leave the script behind and speak off the cuff, from the heart, softly but with a big stick...and any number of other ways that don't involve clichés. You want depth from your speaker, and you'll find out how deep she is by how willing she is to field questions – and to answer those questions with more than prepackaged versions of her own speech. If she's truly an expert on her topic, she should be able to explain the concepts she's sharing when your fellow writers request the details.

The third thing you want from your special speaker is more of a wonderful benefit than a requirement. You want your speaker to be able to provide examples and/or writing exercises. It's one thing for her to say, "Do A, then B, and finally C." It's quite another for her to say, "Here's how I did A, and here's how that got me to B." Again, you want to stay out of that fourth-grade teacher mentality of "Tell the students how it's done." You ought to see how it's done with real-world examples. You want to be able to practice the techniques she's sharing before she leaves.

How writing groups work: The editing

What everything comes down to, however, is the editing. We could talk about pen colors and special speakers all day, but the true point of a writing group is to produce better writers. That is accomplished when writers actually write, print out their stories/articles/chapters, and bring that writing to be read – and edited – by fellow writers. Then the true author takes those critiques, absorbs all the good stuff, kicks out all the irrelevant stuff, and crafts something truly wonderful – a well-edited, oft-revised manuscript that shows off what a true author can really produce when he's pushed to his limit.

Because that's what editing does: it pushes writers to their limit. Editing forces a writer to look at his words through someone else's glasses. He sees his words again for the first time – new, unique, and read by someone who has no idea where the story's going next.

If you don't think that's one of the most important things for a budding writer, let's flash back in time again. It's 1979, and I'm 9 years old. I've just finished my "masterpiece," and my mother – who 20/20 hindsight says was a wonderful editor – asks to read my book.

In fact, she didn't just ask to "read" my book; she asked to edit my book. But I didn't know that in 1979. I thought I was getting back-patting and cheerleading for a job well done. Instead, I got a backside-kick and a "try again" comment. She was pushing me to my limit, telling me I could do better, saying there was one more rung on that ladder to good writing – and I should climb to it.

Writing groups are places exactly like that: places where writers get together to sharpen their skills. We critique each other with the goal of improving our work. The true author takes those critiques and gets better. Freeloading "writers" sit around (like I did for 15 years) and tell themselves, "I'm great!" What the freeloading writer fails to hear is the world's response: "You could be better."

In the next chapter we'll look at four examples of the Good Critiquer – the Mentor we should all strive to be. They're the kinds of people you want in your writing group, the ones who truly want you to grow as an author – the ones who will say, "You can do better." I've seen and worked with each of these Mentors at least once (and usually much more often) in the groups I've attended or led. These people – like my mother – will make comments you don't want to hear, but that's their role in your writing life. These people are the Mentors you want reading your work, not the Freeloaders who say "You're brilliant" even when all you've done is plagiarize the phone book. Let's meet these Mentors so you can seek them out in your writing life.

3 |

The Mentors

The Mentor: Spotting him by his writing

You want the Mentor to edit your writing because that person will tell you what you're doing right as well as what you're doing wrong. The Mentor will offer encouragement, alternatives, and advice. The Mentor is that special somebody you want to read your work.

But how do you tell the difference between the Mentor and the Freeloader? First, look at his own writing and the process he takes to get there. While the writing is not a sure-fire method for spotting Mentors, it's a place to start. Many times, the authors who produce the best writing understand the work involved in the craft. They've not only suffered the long hours at the keyboard, but they've printed out their work, edited it, rewritten it, printed it again, shown it to several Mentors of their own, and revised it once more.

If you're not sure how the writing really reflects the process, go to your local bookstore and peruse the author acknowledgements pages in your favorite genre. You'll see the authors thanking their own critique groups, spouses, agents, or friends – but those people are often described as "my harshest critic" or the people who "helped make this better." Read the books that contain those acknowledgments – all of them.

Now go back to your bookstore and find books where the authors don't mention anyone else helping them edit. There is no "harsh critic" listed in the acknowledgements. Read those books and compare them to the first set. See the differences? I certainly do whenever I do this exercise, and I'm sure you will also.

Now try this exercise: Find a series author; mystery and fantasy are good genres for finding a long-running series. Pick up the first couple books of the series and check the acknowledgements page to find an author who thanks his writing group or critic. Now pick up the last book in the series and see if the writing group or harsh critic has disappeared from the acknowledgments – often, it has. Read the entire series (yes, even if it's 12 books long), and you'll likely see the work start to deteriorate as the writing group and/or harsh critic disappears from the acknowledgments.

Of course, it's not always the case that the writing deteriorates, but it happens often enough that I can usually spot the point at which a Mentor stopped critiquing the author. There are more grammar and punctuation mistakes, the sentences get chunkier, the characters are shallower, and the plot often meanders into oblivion. But reading and critically evaluating another person's writing is often a good indication of whether he's a Mentor you can learn from or a Freeloader you should avoid.

The Mentor: Spotting her by the critiques she takes

The next way to spot the Mentor is to watch the way she accepts critiques of her own material. Is she defensive? Combative? Does she try to justify her mistakes? Or does she accept the critiques as legitimate discussions of her work? Are they opportunities to make improvements to the material and to become a better writer?

Don't make hasty judgments at this point in your search for a Mentor, though. I've discovered that my first impression of the way someone accepts critiques may not be the most accurate.

| 26 |

For example, one man visited my writing group and distributed a chapter from his novel. I edited it, and I don't think there was a paragraph in the entire chapter that I didn't cover with blue ink. Since it was the first work of his I'd ever read, I was apprehensive about giving him my critique. To make matters worse, when the group discussed his chapter, he argued with us. We told him the pacing was too fast – and he argued. We told him that a couple characters needed fleshing out – and he argued. The plot? He argued. The dialogue? He argued. It was one of the roughest critiques I've had to give; I didn't expect him ever to return to our group, and I wasn't sure it would be worth the arguing to critique any of his other stories. That was my first impression.

However, this man returned to our group – with a revised first chapter that incorporated several of our suggestions. I learned that my first impression of him had been inaccurate. While he appeared to argue with us, he was actually forcing us to elaborate on our suggestions, often giving him even more ideas by the fact that we had to overcome his "arguments." We became good friends.

While this man argued (or "discussed," as he liked to say) for the sake of learning, most times people argue for the sake of defending their point. In a writing group, that point may be bad writing, and the arguing is more a waste of time than an opportunity to learn. Watch – and listen – carefully to how people accept critiques, then read their next work to see if they improve. Most often, the people who accept critiques with a certain amount of humility and a "Yes, I see your point" attitude are the ones who are working the hardest to improve their craft. Those are the people most likely to be your Mentors.

The Mentor: Spotting him by the critiques he gives

I can't emphasize this point enough: You can definitely spot a Mentor by the critiques he gives.

Does he tell you that his grandmother wrote better than you when she was in second grade? Does he scribble cutting comments like "Get a real job!" or "You call this writing?" on your manuscript? Does he tell you that your writing will never be as good as his? Then you have found a writing Freeloader. Avoid him.

On the other hand, have you found someone who points out your mistakes and offers suggestions to improve them? Have you found someone who scribbles across your manuscript "Here's what you're doing well – and here's where you can improve"? Have you found someone who encourages you to take that next step toward better writing? Then you have found a Mentor you can trust to help improve your work. Listen to him.

A writing Mentor: The Masseuse

Now that you can recognize a Mentor when you see her, let's discuss a few different ones you're likely to run across.

The first kind of Mentor you might meet is the Masseuse. Professionals in the massage field are trained to find the tension, the scarring, and the knots and to work them out. Here is what I've experienced when receiving a professional back massage:

First, the masseuse takes a towel and lays it across my back. On top of this towel, she places large, heated stones that put warm pressure on various spots such as around my shoulder blades and down my spine. Those heated stones start soaking up the tension, making my back more pliable so that when she removes them she can start right in on the muscles and joints that have been primed for her ministrations.

She kneads the muscles in my shoulders, pulling the tension from my neck and spine. She finds that bit of scar tissue near the left shoulder blade, and she starts breaking it up. I might grimace at the pain, but I don't say anything because it feels so good to have that tissue broken apart – I can actually move my arm a little easier now that she's done that. Next, she moves down my spine, pulling the tension along with her fingers, working out the knots and kinks. I feel like I'm sinking into the table.

She stops, and I can't believe the hour is over. She reminds me to drink plenty of water (at least 40 ounces, preferably 64), and I leave feeling on top of the world. In fact, I haven't felt this good in years.

Where's the literary interpretation?

The Masseuse in your writing group warms you up with praising comments of your writing. She places those warm comments on various parts of your writing that need to be drawn forward. That tricky scene you rewrote until 2 a.m.? That gets a warm comment. The character you worked so hard to flesh out? Another warm comment. Praise, congratulations, and affirmation for a job well done. You did well; now do it some more.

But just as the warm rocks are removed to make way for the real work of the massage, the literary Masseuse moves on to the tension in your manuscript's shoulders and spine. With warm encouragement and unerring accuracy, the Masseuse pulls out every place where your manuscript could be tightened and improved. Her comments pull the tension of your manuscript forward, working through the scar tissue of your incomplete thoughts, rambling sentences, and weak narrative structure.

By the time the Masseuse finishes with your manuscript, you're sinking into your chair and can't believe she's already finished. And her parting thought before you leave? Have a drink. (Water, if that's your preference; something stronger if you feel it's necessary.)

The Masseuse will pinpoint the flaws in your manuscript and work them to the surface where you can finally deal with them. She'll praise what you're doing well and encourage you to keep up the great work. By the time she's through with your manuscript, it'll feel like kneaded dough. But you'll thank her for the insight, the brutal honesty, and the tenacity to keep massaging even when you were wincing at the pain.

A Mentor: The Bookworm

The Bookworm is an author who has read everything. When I say "everything," I'm not exaggerating very much. He read books before he learned to walk. He worked his way through every genre as a weekend diversion to the classics he breezed through in grade school. By high school he was studying medieval literature while reading non-fiction in his spare time.

Even though his cousin is a writing Freeloader (the Student of Writing, discussed in more detail in Chapter 4), the Bookworm is a wonderful Mentor to budding authors. He knows something about almost everything, and he can usually point authors in new (or old) directions. He's read the best and worst that the history of writing has to offer, and he can make suggestions that will point your work toward that which is best.

When you start that new book about vampires, he can tell you if you're writing in the Bram Stoker or Anne Rice tradition – and offer suggestions to make your work better than theirs. When you start that new western, he knows every Louis L'Amour (including the entire Sackett family tree), and he can tell you when your cowboy does something no cowboy in his right mind would ever do.

Not only does the Bookworm know fiction, but he's read every non-fiction book in existence. Because of that, he can point out the perfect book to help you overcome your writing shortcomings, and he can steer you clear of the fluff pieces that would do you more harm than good.

The Bookworm is a wealth of information on a variety of topics, and you should make use of his knowledge. Beware, however, that because he's so well-read he has high expectations for the manuscripts he reads in the group. He's read the classics, and he's read the literary giants. You may be writing a simple gardening book, but he'll expect to feel the dirt oozing between his fingers as he grips your typed pages. You may think that's unfair of him to expect so much from your first draft, but you'll find that the Bookworm is a strong motivator. Few things are more motivating than to have someone say, "You could really learn from reading a few Jane Austen novels." Then ask him which Jane Austen novels and read them.

A Mentor: The Taskmaster

According to Webster's New World Dictionary, a taskmaster is a demanding person who assigns difficult tasks. That is a great description of the Taskmaster in a writing group. Simply put, she expects the most out of everyone. It doesn't matter if the author has been attending the group for 20 years and has 50 novels on the shelf – the Taskmaster wants to know what that author is working on next.

The Taskmaster pushes everyone in the group to achieve more and to achieve it better than they did last time. That comes both in the form of how many words are produced as well as the quality of those words. You say you wrote 5,000 pretty good words this month? Then the Taskmaster will ask for 6,000 great words next month.

The great thing about a Taskmaster attending a writing group is that she keeps everyone else on task. It's easy for writing groups to degenerate into little social clubs where everything is discussed except the writing. The Taskmaster hates that. She knows the group exists to produce better writers, and if she doesn't feel like she's growing with each meeting she attends, she'll get the ruler out and crack a few fingers until people get to business.

As harsh as she sounds, the Taskmaster can be quite inspirational. That's because she expects as much (or more) of herself than she does of others. While she's pushing her fellow writers to produce more and better, she's staying up until the wee hours of the morning click-clacking away on her own keyboard. Her writing is often polished, her character profiles detailed, and her subplots as intricately drawn as the main plot. When she distributes new work to the group, it's often a joy to read and a breeze to edit. If there is anyone aspiring writers can hold up as a role model, the Taskmaster is just that person.

Unfortunately, these fine qualities have their negative sides as well. Sure, the Taskmaster keeps groups from degenerating into social clubs, but she can go overboard with that attitude. A writing group needs to stay on task, but a certain amount of socializing always happens when groups of people get together. Don't let the Taskmaster squelch that natural tendency toward group friendships and bonds. As odd as it may sound to the Taskmaster, writing growth and inspiration can happen when people just sit and chit-chat as well as when they pour sweat over that latest manuscript. A good friend of mine once said that he didn't get his best ideas in his office staring at the computer screen; his best ideas came to him when he went outside and played fetch with his puppy. The Taskmaster has trouble with this concept, and she sometimes must be reigned in or she'll squelch the social dynamic that is also important to a writing group's health and success.

The second cautionary note about the Taskmaster is that, while she can be an inspiration to the budding writer, she also can be quite intimidating. Writers work incredibly hard at their craft, and it's not always that encouraging to hear someone say, "I want more, and I want it better." Newer writers, especially, may hear that and go home thinking, "I don't have what it takes." What the Taskmaster sees as an inspiring goal to achieve may be perceived by the novice writer as an insurmountable wall. The trick for the Taskmaster (and the group as a whole) is to provide that inspiration without drowning the writer's muse, and that's a balancing act the Taskmaster can't always perform.

While the Taskmaster has no nasty relative (like the Bookworm's evil cousin Student of Writing), she can sometimes become her own worst enemy. Work with the Taskmaster(s) of your group to provide the inspiration that all writers desire without the overwhelming obstacles that no writers can overcome. You'll find that the Taskmaster can be a writer's best advocate in the long run.

A Mentor: The College Professor (Dr. Jekyll)

Like Dr. Jekyll and Mr. Hyde, the College Professor has two distinct halves. I'll talk about the Hyde-side in Chapter 5. The Dr. Jekyll side of the College Professor is absolutely brilliant. He's a master of the English language, he's a fantastic teacher who can pinpoint a writer's problem and provide the perfect response, he has an infinite number of ways to explain himself, he never loses patience, and he encourages authors to shoot for the perfect "A."

One of the best things about the College Professor is that he's often an excellent line editor. Line editing means the person reviewed the manuscript line by line for mistakes in grammar, spelling, and punctuation. The better the line editor, the more detailed the marks on the manuscript – and all the more reason to use a color besides red. A really good line editor will also comment on the manuscript's characters, plot, dialogue, and narrative structure.

Being line-edited, however, is probably the scariest thing imaginable for an author. Almost every time I've been line-edited, I've agreed with the suggestions and changes – but it was still painful flipping through page after page of words crossed out, whole paragraphs moved, sentences rewritten, and plot holes circled. It takes a dedicated College Professor to go through all the work involved in line-editing every manuscript that comes through a writing group each month, but it takes an even more courageous author to submit his work to that kind of scrutiny on a regular basis.

The benefits of having a manuscript line-edited far outweigh those few, dreadful minutes of shock at all the ink on the page. When you take the time to review the changes the College Professor made, you'll see the manuscript improved. When you digest those kinds of improvements and make an effort to incorporate them in your everyday writing, then great things will happen. You'll find yourself thinking, "What would the College Professor do here? Can I use that word? Would another phrase be more evocative?"

The College Professor also has a knack for inspiring followers. I've seen groups where one College Professor takes the time to line-edit, and it isn't long before a second and then a third member of the group starts line-editing. That depth of critiquing is contagious, and more group members often try their hand at it. It will feel like any editing session that doesn't run a pen dry wasn't a productive editing session – whether the manuscript is your own or someone else's.

Another benefit of having the College Professor in a group is he's often willing to teach his line-editing skill to anyone willing to try. That means that even those group members who don't learn well through simple imitation can learn the skills to become better editors – and better writers in the process.

One final word on the College Professor: He's not always a literal college professor. This person may not teach as a profession; he may not have attended college. This person could be anyone who has mastered the in-depth editing skills I've described and has the ability to teach and inspire others. That ability could be innate, or he could have gone to school to learn it, or it could be something he's picked up on the job. Don't judge a College Professor by the letters after his name – or by the lack of them.

The good writing group: Knowing it when you see it

This discussion of the Masseuse, the Bookworm, the Taskmaster, and the College Professor should have given you a good idea of the kinds of qualities that make up a successful writing group. The best groups encourage, challenge, support, cheer, and lament.

Writing is a lonely profession, and writers need a certain amount of encouragement. Sometimes that encouragement comes from the writer's family but not always. Even when the writer's spouse, children, parents, and third cousins offer their best support, there's something more that's gained from the encouragement of like-minded individuals, that camaraderie that can only be found when a group of writers sit at a table and throw around ideas. They learn from each other, they grow with each other – they encourage each other.

At the same time, the best writing groups challenge their writers. It's easy for writers to exist within their own little bubble, never venturing outside the safe little books they read and write. When writers get together, though, they start challenging each other with new ideas, new topics, new ways of thinking and writing. The romance author critiques someone's horror novel while the fantasy author picks up the latest mainstream novel because her friend at the meeting said it was a page-turner that everyone should read. This exchange of ideas is challenging to the tired writer – and inevitably helps her grow into a well-rounded individual and into a stronger, more confident writer.

The best writing group members support each other. Because we're all in this game together, we know how hard it can be. When we hear about contests and new markets and nearby conferences, we share that information. Writers help each other whenever possible, pointing out the new magazines, praising the good agents (or warning against the bad ones), and sharing what we learned from editors. That kind of support is necessary these days for writers to succeed – it's always been necessary, but it seems to be more so with each passing year.

And finally, the best writing groups cheer the good fortune and lament the misfortune of their members. Some groups celebrate recent publications with free cups of coffee, while others prefer cookies or applause. The point is that writing group members cheer each other on through the successes – and lament with the writers who stumble along the way. Because no matter how many successes a writer might achieve, any one cutting remark or personal attack can feel like a punch to the gut. That's the time when the really good writing groups shine – when they rally around the bleeding writer, patch her up, and put her back into that chair and ask her to write some more.

Unfortunately, not all writing groups contain the best members to accomplish those goals. In Chapters 4 and 5, I'll tell you about several Freeloaders that every writer should avoid.

4

The Passive Freeloaders

The Freeloader: Spotting him by the critiques he takes

The person you should avoid in a writing group – the Freeloader – is easily spotted by the way he receives critiques.

Start from this perspective: "I do not need to be critiqued." Everything about the Freeloader stems from that statement. He knows what he does well – everything – and he sees little reason to listen to anyone tell him how to write. So, when he distributes new work to the writing group, he's not looking for constructive criticism; he's looking for affirmation. He wants a pat on the back, a "good job," and a book-and-film contract for $100 million. (He's basically me at 9 years old.)

When the other members of the writing group try to critique him, he ignores them. It may not be blatant; he may look like he's giving the other members his undivided attention, but he has no intention of doing anything that's suggested to him. What he's waiting for is the "good stuff." He wants to know that people liked it, that people were drawn in by the characters and pulled forward by the plot. He wants to hear people say, "I can't wait to read what happens next!" – and he'll take up as much of the group's time as he can to explain the rest of the story. At his core, the Freeloader is self-centered, overtly egotistical, and opposed to change of any kind, specifically change that involves more work on his writing.

The Freeloader will take critiques like this: Someone tells him that a sentence would sound better if he changed it this way, and the Freeloader says, "No, I want it to sound like that. It'll become very important 20 pages from now." Someone else will tell him that a character seems too one-dimensional, and the Freeloader will explain that everyone missed the subtle nuances he creatively wove through the character's actions. Someone will point out to him that he misspelled the word "The," and the Freeloader, after careful consideration, will reply with either "The computer must have done that" or "No, I did that on purpose." There is just no convincing him. The best advice is to tell him what you think and move on as quickly as possible. There's no sense wasting valuable time trying to convince the Freeloader that he could be better when he "knows" he's as good as it gets.

The Freeloader: Spotting her by the critiques she gives

The critiques the Freeloader gives are a slightly different matter than the ones she takes. The first mistake you can make is to assume that everything the Freeloader says is worthless. The second mistake is to assume that everything she says is gospel truth. Between worthless and revelation, however, the Freeloader sometimes relates a truth that can benefit your writing. The trick is distilling the good from all the extraneous material she throws at you.

First, let's discuss the kinds of critiques you're likely to receive from a Freeloader. Remember, she believes her work is perfect and everyone else's work could be perfect if they only listened to her. As such, her critiques will likely be dogmatic, preachy, and condescending. She won't give you suggestions for improvement; she'll give you directives. She'll try to convince you that her way is the perfect way to rewrite your work, and she'll convey all of this as if she's doing you a favor, as if she didn't really have to tell you any of it but is doing so just to "help out the little guy."

Most importantly, however, her critiques will come across as the only possible way to revise the manuscript. But please, understand this: Except in cases of grammar, spelling, and punctuation, there are no set rules that writers *must* follow. Even grammar rules are sometimes merely guidelines. For example, the "Rule" is that people should not italicize a character's thoughts – but *Dune*, by Frank Herbert, is filled with italicized thoughts. The "Rule" is that people should write clear, precise narratives with a distinct point of view. But Louis L'Amour wrote his novels as if they were stories told around the campfire. The "Rule" is that people should write in either first or third person, but not in both. Yet James Patterson's *When the Wind Blows* mixes those two through the entire novel. The history of writing is filled with people who successfully broke rules. Don't let your Freeloader tell you there's only one way to write or revise your manuscript.

Having said all that, however, you should be aware that the Freeloader sometimes has important things to say about manuscripts. Sometimes she spots clunky sentences or plot holes, and while she may not convey the information in the most constructive manner, that doesn't mean her points should automatically be ignored. Evaluate her comments apart from her tone and word choice, and see if they're valid. If your Freeloader has a point, then you have an obligation as an informed author to deal with it, whether that requires a minor revision or a complete rewrite. Remember, your job is to make your writing the best it can possibly become. Don't miss any opportunity to improve it, even if that opportunity came from a Freeloader.

The bulk of these next two chapters is reserved for a discussion of nine Freeloaders – nine kinds of people who can get into a writing group and cause no end of trouble. These are the ones who tell you your writing is all wonderful or it's all awful, the ones who eat up the group's time because they crave attention, the ones who soak up everything without ever giving back anything in return.

Each of these Freeloaders, however, also has a good side. As I said, just because someone is a Freeloader doesn't mean you can't learn from her. The trick is figuring out how to get the most out of what she gives you. Step back from the personal insults or the vague generalizations and really interpret what she's saying about your writing. That's not always an easy thing to do, but time often makes it easier, and I'll discuss techniques that work with each Freeloader.

What is a "Passive Freeloader"?

This chapter is called "The Passive Freeloaders," and most of the preceding material describes why I even use the word "Freeloader." But what is this "Passive" thing all about?

Simply put, the Passive Freeloader doesn't actively try to be a Freeloader. She doesn't try to put down her fellow writers, she really wants to help and be a part of the writing group, and she thinks that what she's doing is helping everyone involved. She often has the best intentions, but as the saying goes, the road to Hell is paved with those best intentions.

Before you take me too literally, let me stress that the Passive Freeloader is unlikely to lead a writing group to Hell. She can, however, disrupt the work that a good group is trying to accomplish. As you'll see from my discussion of these three Passive Freeloaders, they either do not participate at all (the Sponge), participate way too much (the Storyteller), or don't participate in a way that is truly beneficial (the Cheerleader).

The Passive Freeloaders should be carefully watched when they're part of a group, but their foibles can often be circumvented by an effective leader and a willing membership. The best part about Passive Freeloaders is that, with a little time and effort, they can often become fully productive members of a strong and healthy group. They can even become Mentors and successful authors, which is the best result we want for all writing group members.

A Freeloader: The Sponge

I start with the Sponge because he's probably one of the least bothersome Freeloaders in a writing group. While the rest of the group discusses, analyzes, critiques, and edits, the Sponge sits there and soaks it all in. He watches and listens and – I assume – learns, but he never gives any of that back to the group. He might write, but no one's ever seen any evidence of it. He collects the manuscripts that everyone distributes, but he brings them back almost as pristine as he received them, the bent corners the only evidence that he actually read them. Essentially, the Sponge is a warm body to fill out the group's attendance numbers.

Unlike the lump that he resembles at the end of the table, a Sponge who attends a writing group for any period of time will learn. He will soak up the knowledge from everyone else, and his writing will likely improve. Unfortunately, he never takes full advantage of the opportunities available in a writing group setting. Since he sits there silently, people might rarely (if ever) speak to him. Since no one sees any evidence that he's learning, people might never ask his thoughts on issues. Since no one asks him to participate in the discussion, he misses out on even more opportunities to learn, and – the saddest part about a Sponge attending a group – the gap between what he knows and what he *could know* grows wider.

The real problem with a Sponge attending a writing group is actually not the damage he does to the group (which is often minimal), but it is the damage he does to himself. The Sponge could be so much more than he is, but he doesn't grow to his fullest potential because he never interacts; he never practices the editing techniques that he sees everyone else using. It could be that he's naturally shy, or maybe he's intimidated by all the people he thinks are professionals in the group (even if they've also never published anything).

A Sponge does little damage to individual writers either, unless the Sponge is a writer's only editor. As long as a writer has several Mentors in his life to offset the Sponge's silence, there's little the Sponge does to harm his fellow writer. One-on-one, he may say a little more about a manuscript than he would in a group setting, but that's still very little. Considering the Sponge's unwillingness to talk to the group, those few sentences may not be as informative as a writer would like. Whatever his reason, he's causing the most damage to himself.

However, it would be a mistake to underestimate a Sponge's potential. Silent is entirely different from knowing nothing. (If that sounds blatantly obvious, ask yourself this: How often is the most verbose person in any group considered the most knowledgeable, even if he knows nothing? Sadly, far too often.) The Sponge may not share what he knows, and there are likely times when he doesn't know an answer, but don't assume he has nothing to contribute. The more you talk to him and get him to participate, the more likely he is to become a fully integrated member of a writing group.

However, there are two worst-case scenarios for a Sponge. The first is that the Sponge leaves without really learning anything about the writing and editing process. This is the saddest thing for the Sponge himself, because he will probably feel that his time was wasted and that he got nothing out of the group. He may continue writing, or he may decide that he was "never meant to be a writer." Either way, however, the writing group he attended probably won't remember him after a couple meetings – sadly.

The second worst-case scenario is that the Sponge attends the writing group for years but never shares his knowledge. This may happen because the group doesn't let him or because he decides he has nothing to share. This is the saddest thing to happen to the entire group, because the Sponge could be such a benefit to the group. A perceptive group leader may be able to coax this Sponge into participating, but some

Sponges remain resolute in their determination never to participate. My advice for dealing with this kind of Sponge: Never stop trying. If the Sponge doesn't want to participate, he won't; but if he's encouraged often enough, he might turn into a fully-participating member of the writing group.

When the Sponge finally wrings out some of that pent-up knowledge, be ready for a deluge. The Sponge may have waited months (or even years) to begin expressing himself – and that expression might come slowly – but when it comes, the Sponge will surprise everyone with his insights. His new writing will incorporate all the best suggestions from the group, and his critiques will display a wonderful level of perception.

A Freeloader: The Cheerleader

The second Freeloader is similar to the Sponge in that she does little damage to a writing group as long as she's countered by good Mentors. However, the Cheerleader can be quite damaging to the revision process when she's the only voice a writer hears – or the only voice that a writer wants to hear.

The Cheerleader in a writing group is exactly what her name implies: She stands on the sidelines of the writing game and cheers the players forward no matter how bad the score. Weak modifiers, brilliant plots, flat characterization, scintillating dialogue – it doesn't matter because they all get cheered.

To be fair, the Cheerleader honestly wants every writer to succeed, and she believes it is her duty to cheer those writers on until they finally achieve success. The problem with that strategy, though, is that it doesn't involve anything beyond the cheering. The Cheerleader has nothing to offer the writer in terms of strategy, composition, development, or style. She believes that writers only succeed when they're praised for their efforts, so she takes it upon herself to praise everything that writers write. The cheering can be okay when the writer's written something to cheer about, but that's not always the case.

By herself, one lone Cheerleader does little damage to an entire writing group of Mentors. Everyone needs encouragement to keep moving forward, and the Cheerleader certainly provides that. In fact, she can be a nice counter-balance in an overly critical writing group. When everyone else is marking up the manuscript with their blue pens, it's a life-saving breath for a writer to hear a simple, "I enjoyed it." I've been in meetings where exactly that has happened. Often when the Cheerleader praises the work, the overly critical people will suddenly realize how harsh their words sounded and offer praise of their own. The Cheerleader reminds the group that writers need praise, and that's incredibly important.

However, there are two real problems for a group with a Cheer-leader. The first problem occurs when the Cheerleader strives so hard to find something to praise that she ends up praising material that doesn't deserve it. If the dialogue is bad and the Cheerleader says it's good, then the writer may never learn to write better dialogue. The same can be said of any other portion of a manuscript, such as the characters, narrative, plot, research, etc. While encouragement is always needed, genuinely constructive criticism is vital. Giving a writer nothing but encouragement only gives her the support she needs to jump off the cliff – with a smile on her face.

The second problem for a group with a Cheerleader happens when the writer receives the kind of constructive criticism she needs to im-prove, but instead of following that advice, she listens only to the Cheer-leader and believes the work is perfect the way it is. She never revises the manuscript because the Cheerleader "loved it." Again, think of me at 9 years old. I had one editor telling me everything I didn't want to hear. If I'd had a second editor telling me my book was great, I would have had "evidence" that my mother was wrong. Instead, I was forced to confront the possibility she might be right.

A Freeloader: The Storyteller

Writers love to tell stories. Even non-fiction writers live for the final draft, that final story that conveys a point to the audience. It's ingrained in us as wordsmiths, that desire to tell others about the highs and lows happening in our world. As children, we observed our neighborhoods and collected the bits and pieces of stories happening around us. Those snatches of life became the news reports we told around the dinner table, the tall tales we used to scare our siblings, and the kernels of plots that became our favorite short stories.

Unfortunately, that same storytelling propensity gets writers into trouble when they don't know when to stop. That's the case with the third Freeloader, the Storyteller.

In a writing group, a Storyteller can be quite disruptive. His desire to tell the story is so all-consuming that he doesn't know when to stop – and if no one else stops him, he can even take up an entire meeting. Yes, I've seen it happen. (I allowed it to happen in one of my earliest meetings as a leader, so please learn from my mistake.) His story might be interesting, and he might even have wonderful insights on life and the business of writing. It's even possible that the Storyteller inspires someone to craft short stories from the tales he relates. The problem is that the writing group meeting is not the proper forum for all this storytelling.

The Storyteller won't do much harm to any individual writer, but he will harm the overall effectiveness of the writing group. The Storyteller has the potential to distract the group from its goal, to divert constructive discussions on editing toward irrelevant conversations on anything but writing. Most writing groups have limited time in which to do their work. People have jobs and families to consider, bookstores and libraries have closing times to enforce, and visitors (and regular members too) will feel their time was wasted if one person monopolizes the meeting for personal story time.

When a Storyteller attends a group, someone (preferably the leader) must work extra hard to keep the discussion on task. Set a specific time when the meeting begins and make sure everyone knows when the meeting should end, then enforce a ban on extraneous conversations during the meeting. Encourage people to show up early and to stay late so they can chat during those times instead of during the meeting. If all else fails, interrupt the Storyteller's story before he gets too far into it and tell him to save it for later. The worst thing for the writing group would be for the Storyteller's story to eat up the entire meeting so that nothing gets critiqued. Yes, that can happen. It's one of the most aggravating things for a group leader.

The Storyteller can be the most disruptive, however, when he's not a regular member of the group. Often, a Storyteller will visit a writing group just to have a new bunch of people with whom he can share his latest story. I have little patience for a visiting Storyteller. Too often I've seen him attend one meeting, eat up precious time with stories he "knows" everyone wants to hear, and then never return. This is the height of egotism, and the visiting Storyteller knows that most people are too polite to stop him before he's done his damage.

Writing groups typically have so few members attending that any visitor is granted a certain amount of privilege, and the visiting Story-teller takes unfair advantage of that privilege. The group members hope any visitor will return, but the longer the Storyteller tells his stories, the more the members wish he'd just go away. There's a collective sigh of relief when the visiting Storyteller does not return, but by then he's al-ready done his damage. The group is behind schedule, truly productive conversations were squelched, and the group is much more skittish the next time a visitor drops by.

The visiting Storyteller is a much more difficult Freeloader to deal with because there's the underlying hope that he'll return and reform into a productive member – and because people tend to want to be nice to strangers. Don't let that become the overriding consideration, though. If the visiting Storyteller returns, he'll benefit most from understanding the rules right away. If he starts taking the meeting off track, gently guide him back to the topic. If he refuses to be guided, take a firmer grip on the conversation – and yes, that might offend him. But if he understands from his first meeting that the group is serious about its editing and critiquing tasks (and that there is ample time before and after the meeting for general chit-chat), then he'll be more likely to become a long-term, productive member than a nuisance that everyone barely tolerates.

In the next chapter, I'll talk about six Active Freeloaders. They're the Freeloaders who can seriously injure a writer, the ones who actively seek their own affirmation at the expense of all others. I'll also discuss how to deal with Freeloaders when they attend a writing group. There are strategies you can employ to help them grow into the kinds of Mentors who will really help you grow as an author.

5

The Active Freeloaders

What is an "Active" Freeloader?

You learned about Passive Freeloaders in the previous chapter and met three of the most common ones. While a Passive Freeloader seldom overtly hinders a writing group (the Storyteller can be an exception), an Active Freeloader can do real and extensive harm to her fellow writers. This is the kind of Freeloader I described at the beginning of this book, the one who inflates her ego at the expense of someone else. She has no reservations about telling you how much she knows that you do not. Her comments will sting, her critiques will be personal, and her attacks will be unflinching. The Active Freeloader is a writer's worst enemy.

This Freeloader can believe her actions are in the best interests of the writer, and that's one of the things that makes her most dangerous. Like her relatives, the Passive Freeloaders, she believes that she can help her writer friends, and she does it by the worst possible means. She may never realize the damage she causes, and she may leave a trail of broken writers in her wake, but she presses on exactly as she has because of a mistaken belief that her methods work.

It takes conviction and a strong leader for a writing group to counter the effects of an Active Freeloader. Her critiques will appear legitimate, but they'll display an underlying sense of hostility toward and disdain for her fellow writer. Her comments (both written and verbal) must be interpreted with an understanding that she doesn't really care about the writer as much as she claims. When she starts making overly critical comments, stop her. When she starts making personal attacks, tell her they won't be tolerated. Do not allow her to destroy her fellow writers.

This chapter is devoted to a discussion of six Active Freeloaders. These are the people you do not want reading your manuscript, and if you find yourself on the receiving end of one of their critiques, you must understand never to take their remarks personally. Several of them can display good qualities, and I'll discuss those as well, but most of them can do extensive damage. It's best to be aware of these people now so you know how to deal with them when you come across them in the wild.

A Freeloader: The Egotist

The Egotist is probably the simplest Freeloader to explain: He believes no one in the world writes better than he does. It doesn't matter how good your manuscript; it will never measure up to his work. If you're really "lucky," he'll pull out examples from his own work to prove how much better he is. His expressed reason, of course, is to provide an example of whatever technique he's mastered that the other writer has not, and the best example can only come from his own writing because he's never found anyone who does it better.

He may have actually mastered whatever tidbit of wisdom he's sharing, but his method of sharing is so condescending that the lesson gets lost. He sneers at other opinions. He chuckles when people offer alternatives to his suggestions, as if to say that all other alternatives will result in an inferior manuscript. He hurriedly scribbles his critiques across the manuscript to imply that the other writer should have figured things out already, as if to say, "I can't believe you're still making THIS mistake!"

The Egotist can be quite damaging to a writing group and to individual writers. After receiving enough of these condescending remarks, other writers will feel discouraged. They'll start believing the Egotist when he says they "should know these things already," and they'll start believing that inner voice of doubt when it says, "You're not a *real* writer." They'll stop attending the group, they'll stop writing, and they'll start believing that this whole writing thing just isn't for them.

The Egotist won't care about any of that, though. As far as he's concerned, if those so-called writers couldn't make it playing with the big dogs, then they had no business playing at all. The literary establishment (of which he will proudly proclaim to be a member) is better off without them. The people who remain in the writing group are the ones who have been through the fire and deserve to be there, the ones who really could tough it out – the true literati.

In actuality, the people who remain are usually one of two kinds of people: Either they are Egotists themselves, or they are staying with the group because they have the fortitude to stand up beneath the onslaught and still try to improve their writing. Either way, however, the damage has already been done, both to the group and to the other writers.

A writing group comprised of Egotists actually has a more narrow focus on writing than they believe. Because Egotists run off anyone who does not measure up to their standards of perfection, they end up with a group of people who write and think exactly as they do – or who do not voice an opposing opinion on writing for fear of being cut down. That single perspective on writing, where the Egotist never has to defend or explain himself, limits his ability as a writer.

An Egotist considers it a waste of time to always explain grammar and punctuation rules to new writers. Without him realizing it, though, he's actually helping himself to become a better writer when he launches into those explanations. When he expounds on characterization, dialogue, research – topics he believes he's "covered to death" – he's not only helping the one writer, but he's helping all the other members of the group who suffer from the same problem, and he's helping himself by verbalizing something that may come naturally to him. The simple act of explaining the writing process helps him grow as a writer.

Without those "lower class" writers to explain to, however, the Egotist never has this opportunity to grow. The Egotist never sees this benefit, though. He only perceives a waste of time, a redundant conversation, and a fellow writer who "just doesn't get it."

But what is a writing group to do when confronted by an Egotist? First, don't allow his condescending attitude to infect any other members of the group. Like the worst kind of virus, his egotistical attitude can spread and infect the entire group until all members believe they hold the secret key to literary success. This kind of attitude must be stopped in its tracks. The success of a writing group is based on the exchange of ideas and knowledge so that everyone learns from everyone else.

If the Egotist refuses to settle down, the group's leadership may be forced to resort to drastic action. In all the years I've attended or led writing groups across the country, I've never had to kick out a member, but I've always known the possibility exists. The Egotist can be one of the most damaging influences on a writer and a group, and if he will not temper his comments and direct his critiques at the manuscript instead of the writer, expulsion from the group may be necessary. That kind of action requires strong leadership and the support of a strong, healthy group, but it can be done.

Remember, the health of the group and the livelihood of its members is more important than continually stroking the Egotist's overbearing pride.

A Freeloader: The Nit-Picker

According to my trusty Webster's New World dictionary, a nit is the egg of a louse. As if that wasn't explicit enough, good ol' Webster goes on to tell me that "louse" is more of a common name for a variety of small, wingless insects that feed on human blood and tissue. Sort of shines a new light on the phrase, "Don't be so nit-picky," doesn't it?

My point, though, is that nits are mighty small. People don't usually stumble across nit eggs; they have to hunt for them.

In some ways, the Nit-Picker really is a Mentor. She scours the manuscript for every possible problem that may exist. Big or small, repetitious or singular – she'll spot them all for the writer. The problem with the Nit-Picker, however, is not that she's excellent at spotting nits. The problem is that she wants to show off every last one to the rest of the group.

When it comes time to discuss a manuscript, the Nit-Picker will start with the first word of the first sentence on the first page, pointing out every possible problem in elaborate detail until she reaches the end of the work – or until someone mentions to her that it's nearing midnight. Plot holes and misplaced commas receive the same attention with no regard for which is the more disastrous to the manuscript. It also doesn't matter to her how many times she's pointed out the same kind of mistake because she perceives each one as a special situation instead of a simple variation of a repetitive problem. Her editing time tends to sound like this: "In this sentence you need a comma. Do you see that? And this sentence here – again, a comma. Now in this sentence over here, you used a semicolon, but that really should have been a comma."

Every one of the Nit-Picker's comments could be valid (and often are), but her inability to prioritize her critiques eats up valuable time in which the group could be accomplishing much more. Think back to my 5 Levels of Writing from Chapter 1. At the low end of the continuum exists the misspelled words and rambling sentences. At the high end exists evocative sentences and powerful verbs. Now suppose that the author being critiqued is, overall, a Level 4 writer. She writes with good sentences and solid descriptions, but her details aren't vibrant. Her writing is good, but it doesn't crackle. While we're creating this author, let's give her one more little quirk: She often misspells that nefarious little word "the." Specifically, her fingers fly too fast on the keyboard, and she often transposes the letters so that they come out "hte."

This author knows about her little "hte" quirk, her friends in the writing group know about it, and she knows that she'll have to go back through her manuscript and correct it all the way through – easily done with her computer's find-and-replace function, but still an annoyance.

This author's biggest problem, however, is her lack of vibrant writing. She's technically accurate in everything she writes, but her characters lack deep emotion, her settings seem dull, and her plots are stretched a little too thin.

Enter the Nit-Picker. She reads this author's first chapter and spots 30 times in which the word "the" is misspelled, as well as a character who could be more fully developed, and a hole in the plot. Because every nit deserves equal attention, however, she flips the pages of the chapter and points out to the author each instance in which "the" is misspelled, as well as that one place on page 5 where the main character seemed flat and that other paragraph on page 8 where the plot hole showed up. So, while the author knows that her characters and plot need hard work, the Nit-Picker wastes valuable time pointing out all 30 misspellings when she could have simply said, "You misspelled the word 'the' several times. Fix it."

As I said earlier, the Nit-Picker really can be a Mentor when her detailed line-editing is seriously reviewed by the author. What makes her a Freeloader is her ability to waste meeting time focusing on every little problem within a manuscript as if those problems all deserved equal attention. They seldom do.

The Nit-Picker needs to take the author's ability into perspective when she discusses the manuscript's problems. It's one thing to tell a first-time author that spelling is important to a manuscript's success (she's probably never faced a bored first reader who's looking for an excuse to reject manuscripts), but it's quite another to spend 15 minutes reiterating the merits of good spelling to a multi-published author who mastered spelling (but not typing) years ago and needs much more work on her characters and plot. That's 14 minutes in which the group could have focused on the issues really plaguing the author instead of listening to a litany of misspelled "the's."

A Nit-Picker is usually curbed by a strong group leader willing to stop her before she gets the group too far off track. The biggest damage she can cause to a writing group is to eat up valuable time focusing on trivial issues. Usually a quick reminder of when the store or library closes is enough to get a Nit-Picker to hurry things along. If subtlety doesn't work, then point out to the Nit-Picker that she really is picking nits and the group should focus on the more important issues the author needs to worry about. If the Nit-Picker still won't cooperate, institute a time limit on verbal critiques, and the leader might even bring along a kitchen timer so that everyone stays on task. The Nit-Picker is usually not alone in letting time run away as she speaks, and few things are more motivating than a little timer ticking away the remaining seconds. Once the group gets into the habit of staying on task, the kitchen timer can disappear.

A Freeloader: The Student of Writing

Writers are a huge market for self-help books, classes, and conferences. Scan the magazine rack of your favorite bookstore, and you'll see at least a handful of writing magazines and probably more. Most bookstores devote a couple shelves for writing books, and the larger chain stores fill most of a small aisle. Writer's Digest is a famous publisher of writing books on a variety of topics, and writing books are also published by HarperCollins, Scholastic, Simon and Schuster – there are even Dummies books on everything from grant writing to fiction writing to cover letter formatting.

Writing conferences are held across the country, many of which offer sessions with published authors, agents, and editors. Attendees can meet with those people in short, private sessions or listen to them speak in larger classroom settings. Some of those conferences cover several days, while others start early in the morning and end before lunch.

All of those opportunities for self-improvement have the unfortunate effect of creating a Freeloader called the Student of Writing. The Student of Writing buys every single writing book, attends every conference that comes within 500 miles of his hometown, takes every writing course offered by his local college, and has one bookcase reserved for the autographed books he's collected from every published author he's ever met. The only thing the Student of Writing hasn't done is...write.

The Student of Writing may have been forced to crank out a couple manuscripts for those creative writing courses he took; he probably completed the writing exercises they made him begin at those conferences; and he may have even started several dozen short stories, novels, or articles throughout the years. But he's never had the focus to actually complete any of those orphaned projects.

To the Student of Writing, the exciting aspect of writing is whatever he's doing next. That next thing could be reading another writing book, attending another conference, or writing another novel – but it's never exciting enough for him. The Student of Writing's excitement doesn't come from the "writing" part of his name but from the "student" part of his name. He's perpetually studying, practicing, learning – but never venturing into the real world to put his knowledge into practice.

An alternate personality of the Student of Writing also exists, and he has a tad more focus. This alternate personality is determined to write the Great American Novel. Unfortunately, each new book/conference/class only serves to point out to him how inadequate his current effort really is, and he starts over after completing 50 pages, or he endlessly revises whatever he's already written. The end result is always the same, however: a collection of half-completed manuscripts.

Oddly enough, the Student of Writing is usually an eternal optimist. All of this starting over and endlessly revising and doing things differently seldom discourages him. He sees each new book/conference/class as another inspiration to make his writing that much better, and he's even more excited about the prospect of starting over and turning his Great American Novel into the Greatest American Novel Ever Written.

Unfortunately, all of those books/conferences/classes also turn the Student of Writing into a Freeloader. The Student of Writing has mastered the art of Act I. He can write introductions, prologues, and Chapter 1's that mesmerize readers. He can even write short stories that hold together decently well for probably 2/3 of the way. However, he has no idea how to bring together a satisfying climax or round out a concluding chapter.

Furthermore, the Student of Writing knows very little about final-draft revisions or market submissions. Since he's completed so few manuscripts, he doesn't know how to go back through an entire piece and revise it from the beginning. He's learned several techniques for the process from all his books/conferences/classes, but he's never put them into practice on his own material. As to market submissions, the entire concept is only a vague abstraction to him. He knows what he should do, he's probably even reviewed copies of the "Literary Market Place" or "Writer's Market," and he's got the Google link highlighted, but he's never had the opportunity to submit his own work – or he only submitted a few stories and had no success.

What makes the Student of Writing such a Freeloader is not his lack of experience but the fact that he believes he knows so much. All of those books/conferences/classes have given the Student of Writing a false sense of knowledge. Combine that with all the articles, short stories, and novels that he's started (but never finished), and the Student of Writing's also gained a false sense of experience. He thinks he knows how to write because he's read all about it, and he thinks he's mastered the techniques because he's started so many manuscripts.

Even though nothing's been published (and little has even been completed), the Student of Writing has a catalog of titles he can refer to when discussing any topic. "Well, when I was writing 'The Seventh Voyage of Sinclair' a couple years ago, this is how I developed the story," he says as the topic turns to plotting. Or, as the group begins to discuss dialogue, the Student of Writing jumps in and says, "I remember I had some trouble with dialogue when I wrote, 'Sinclair's Modern Voyage' just last year. Let me tell you how I handled that."

The truth of the matter, though, is that the Student of Writing is hampered by his own love of the student's lifestyle. He's having so much fun learning about writing and about the writing life that he doesn't want to get out and live it. Like the 32-year-old college student who's working on his fourth degree, the Student of Writing refuses to graduate from the student lifestyle. There's always one more book to read, one more conference to attend, and one more class to take, and he never notices how all this learning actually impedes his ability to write.

Before you get the notion to put down this particular writing book and decide to never attend another conference or writing class again, let me stress that these aspects of the writing life are important. Writers grow because of these opportunities and experiences, and there's value to them all. The books instruct writers on topics they know nothing about (whether that's plotting techniques or manuscript submissions); the conferences provide opportunities to interact with agents, editors, and other writers in a safe and supportive environment; and the college writing courses provide guided instruction on techniques that are better learned from a professor and practiced under someone else's guidance. All of those are necessary to a maturing author.

The Student of Writing, however, takes that to the extreme, living the lessons as if they were the life. He lives the writing life vicariously through all the books and classes he attends, believing that those things (and that Great American Novel he's begun 20 times in the past five years) make him a real writer. What makes someone a real writer, however, is his ability to write, not the number of conferences he attends.

The Student of Writing *indirectly* harms the writing group and the individual members. He doesn't believe he's perfect (like the Egotist), and he doesn't get hung up on the insignificant details (like the Nit-Picker). In fact, the Student of Writing is usually as enthusiastic about other people's writing as he is his own, and he's often willing to share his knowledge with anyone who will listen. The problem with the Student of Writing is that he has no real-world experience to round out all that book learning.

This problem goes back to what I said earlier about the rules of writing. The books tell you to do it this way (the "rule"), but the reality is it can actually be done several different ways. For example, the books say that plots must be ordered a certain way so the audience doesn't get lost – but of the millions of books available, there are hundreds (if not thousands) of different ways to organize a plot. The books tell you that dialogue must be done a certain way, but I could spend 15 minutes in a bookstore and easily find an armful of books that break that rule.

I recall the first time I read a Louis L'Amour novel, "The Haunted Mesa." While his fans are quick to point out that's not one of his typical westerns, it was the first L'Amour novel that interested me (I'm not a devoted fan of the Western genre). I complained from start to finish about all the rules L'Amour broke in his writing. The plot didn't move like it was supposed to, the dialogue irritated me, and his narrative technique "wasn't right." I can now see, though, where I had too much of the Student of Writing inside me to really learn from L'Amour.

While he may not have written the way I thought he should have, L'Amour communicated his story in such a way that I can still vividly recall so many details from it – and that's the point the Student of Writing misses. An author does not succeed because he tells stories the way they "should" be told; he succeeds because he *effectively communicates* his story *to his audience*. Think back over all the novels you've read. Which ones left the biggest impressions? Which stories made you fall in love with the characters or bite your nails at the tension or stay up until 3 a.m. because you just had to know what happened next? Was it the ones that followed every rule of storytelling perfectly, or was it the ones that broke a few rules to more effectively convey the story?

A good friend of mine who's a professor in Minnesota says it best. According to her, it's a simple matter of the R.O.T. – or the Rules Of Thumb. People must know the rules of thumb for any industry. The books/conferences/classes are perfect for teaching those rules. After learning the rules, however, a writer must learn to play with them, to figure out which ones should (or even can) be broken. Some are set in stone (such as the proper use of a period), while others are much more malleable (such as the proper way to handle dialogue).

Even the rules I'm giving you in this book can be broken by someone adept enough in the craft of leading a writing group. Just because I tell you that the writing groups succeed when people read the stories silently instead of aloud doesn't mean that a well-functioning writing group couldn't exist in which the members read their stories aloud to each other. I've communicated my "rules" to you, but now that I've done that, I expect two things to happen. First, you'll put my rules of thumb into practice as I've written them, and second, you'll experiment with my rules to determine which ones must be followed, which ones can be bent, and which ones can be outright broken.

Because as my professor/friend in Minnesota says, if you learn the rules of thumb and follow them religiously, then you're doomed to *rot* in the industry. The rules exist to provide a basis from which to begin, but every author worth reading has learned the difference between the rules he must follow and the rules he will follow only in certain situations. The Student of Writing hasn't learned that. To him, the rules must always be followed.

A Freeloader: The Published Writer

The Student of Writing's close cousin is the Published Writer. Where the Student of Writing has published nothing, the Published Writer has published everything – or so it seems. She's either had several short stories published, or she's had her first one or two novels published, and she may have even received glowing reviews from critics, online reviews, and/or social media.

Few writers successfully publish their early work. Even fewer achieve any kind of success with their first novel. There are a certain number of words a writer must write before she can truly call herself a word-smith – an author in the best sense of the word. I put that number somewhere around a million words, but some authors hit their stride sooner than that.

The problem the Published Writer faces is that she's achieving publishing success before she's written enough words to really master her craft. In those first 100,000 or 200,000 words – essentially, her first two or three novels – she's still learning how to fit together a decent plot, how to weave subplots into the overall theme of the story, how to write dialogue that truly sparkles instead of words that only advance the story. Revision and rewriting may still be foreign concepts to her in that early, fevered stage of writing from her gut.

Because that's what many writers do in the early stages of their writing: They write from the gut. The Published Writer, for example, probably wrote that first, published novel because she felt she had to do it. The story was deep inside her, personal and vastly important. It could have sprung from her experiences or from hundreds of hours of research, or maybe she had the story swimming through her head since she was a little girl. Either way, the story was important to her; it was that baby that most writers describe as their completed manuscript.

More real growth happens in the second and third manuscripts, though, because that's when the author has to move beyond the story that must be told to the story that she really wants to tell. Those later stories are equally important to her, but they're more challenging (and therefore a further stretch of her writing muscles) because instead of the words flowing freely out of her in a rush of must-writes, the words grow more organically in a steady flow of will-writes. She must use that first manuscript (indeed, those first million words) to grow as an author, to learn how to weave together the story elements that seemed so natural at first into something that has greater depth and meaning, not only to her but to the reader as well.

The Published Writer achieves publishing success before she has a chance to experience those first million words, and that leads her to believe she knows exactly what she's doing. She may claim humility, but she finds it nearly impossible to practice. After all, she's made it. She's hit the big time. She's sitting on the shelf right next to big dogs like J.K. Rowling, David McCullough, James Patterson, Nora Roberts, C.S. Lewis, and George R.R. Martin.

All of this publicity and notoriety makes the Published Writer vastly important to the members of a writing group, both from her own perspective and from theirs – and that's also what makes her so dangerous.

Before I go any further in this discussion, I must clarify an important difference. Note that this Freeloader is called the Published Writer, not the Published Author. That may sound like an arbitrary distinction, but it's important to my definitions. Recall that I said an author is a person who understands that writing is work. She may possess a certain amount of talent, but she knows where that talent ends and her real work begins. She understands that everything she writes is up for re-vision – nothing is perfect on the first draft. In fact, very little is perfect on the second or third drafts, and the manuscript may not be ready for anyone outside the family to read until it reaches draft 10, if even then. The published author has put in the work, written those first million words, and acknowledged that she had to work hard to produce her manuscript.

I also need to clarify a point here: before you begin worrying about those first million words I've mentioned, keep two things in mind. First, the "rules" I've stated are more like guidelines. Maybe you need a million words, maybe it's two million – or maybe it's only 200,000. Everyone advances at a different pace; you might hit your stride early, or you might need years to hone your craft. Second, even though "one million" sounds like a large number, that's only about 10 novels. For perspective, Ray Bradbury's *The Martian Chronicles* contains about 70,000 words; the first Harry Potter book about 77,000 words; *Sense*

& Sensibility about 120,000 words; *Dune* about 180,000 words; and the first Game of Thrones novel about 300,000 words. The point to remember is that you're using that early writing to improve your craft, and you should see yourself getting better with every short story, every novella, every novel that you write. At some point you'll realize that your writing has improved dramatically and that you've reached that next level.

The Published Writer, however, achieved too much success too quickly. Since she got published immediately, she believes everyone can be published immediately. Since her manuscript received so much praise, she believes she did everything perfectly. Sure, a couple critics may have commented on a plot hole or two, or maybe a fellow writer mentioned that the dialogue could have been tighter, but those kinds of comments wash right off her in the glow of her own success.

Her attitude reminds me of an experience I had in college. My professor required two papers by the end of the course, and he told us how to write them. I wrote the first paper, and I got it back with a 96 percent – an A. He told me to beef up a couple sections, so I wrote the second paper exactly like the first, making sure to put more effort into those areas he mentioned. I got the second paper back with a C- and a scathing critique of my writing ability. Not only had I written the second paper incorrectly, but I had blatantly ignored my professor's instructions. You see, I had written that first paper wrong, too, and he was just being nice to me on that one. But I had been so thrilled by my initial success (an A, after all!), that I had failed to see what I was doing wrong to make the corrections for the second paper.

That is the Published Writer in a nutshell. Simply put, she doesn't know nearly as much as she thinks she knows, but her initial success (her A on that first published manuscript) leads her to believe that's how it's always done. So, she tells everyone how she did it, she writes her next 100,000 words exactly like the last 100,000 words, and she falls flat the second time around.

Unfortunately, the Published Writer can be a writing group's undoing without anyone realizing why. Everyone can see the Published Writer's success – after all, it's her book on the shelf right next to Stephen King's latest bestseller. She obviously did something right, so the group should certainly listen to her. As if that wasn't enough, when she speaks to the group, she speaks with the unerring confidence of a voice of authority. She's probably worked with an agent and a publisher and an editor – she knows what's happening in the inner sanctum of the publishing temple. To further confirm her status as an uber-author, she probably has an agent, editor, and publisher eagerly awaiting that next novel. Who else in the writing group can make such a claim?

That combination of inexperience, notoriety, and self-assuredness is a recipe for writing group disaster. The Published Writer doesn't realize how much she doesn't know. The group members assume she knows what she's talking about, and everyone listens to this naïve voice. The Published Writer's rush of success instills a false sense of immediate gratification in the other members who start believing all that hard work (you know, the boring revisions) must not be necessary for them because it wasn't necessary for the Published Writer.

Members caught up in the glow of the Published Writer's success find themselves rushing through first drafts and calling those drafts complete. They take their manuscripts to the group – but not to hear what everyone says needs improvement. They want to hear only what the Published Writer says, and too often she doesn't have the experience to make a qualified evaluation. (Remember, the success of a writing group depends more on the interaction of various perspectives and levels of experience, not on a cult of the Published Writer's personality.) Members stop caring what any of the Mentors have to say, especially the harsher ones such as the Taskmaster and the (good) College Professor. They only have ears for the wisdom dispensed by the Published Writer.

As I said, though, the Published Writer often falls flat that second time around. Because her initial success was based on a combination of gut reaction and years of plot development while she worked her day job, the Published Writer has trouble producing work of that same quality again. She grasps the first plot that comes to mind (often a cliché, but she doesn't realize that), sits at her keyboard and bangs out that next manuscript in record time (without giving it even a week to percolate in her mind), immediately mails it to her agent or editor, and tells the group how wonderful it is to be a Published Writer.

Of course, any agent or editor worth the money will recognize the slipshod job in the first few pages. One of three things usually happens at that point: 1) the editor/agent returns the manuscript for major revisions, and the Published Writer humbly complies (thereby proving that she's actually on the road to becoming an excellent author); 2) the editor/agent returns the manuscript for major revisions, but the Published Writer holds her ground (after all, she's the one with talent – "If that editor or agent had any real talent," the Published Writer says, "then she'd be a writer like me!"); 3) the manuscript gets thrown into the pipeline for publication as-is, and the editor and agent hope the book achieves at least marginal success and that the writer doesn't screw up as much the next time out – assuming there even is a next time. And unless the first book was a runaway bestseller, the third option is unlikely to occur.

The writing group with a Published Writer in attendance will have a tough time reining her in. It's hard not to get caught up in the excitement of a published manuscript and the sudden notoriety that goes with it – both for the writer as well as the writing group. (Even harder if the writer includes on her acknowledgements page a thank-you note to that very same writing group.) But the members (and especially the group leader) must resist the awe this newfound fame brings with it. The Published Writer is still only one member of the group – she is still one voice, expressing one opinion, and she should not be treated as a sudden authority on all things publishable.

That is best done by equalizing the amount of time she critiques with that of everyone else. If the members each get four minutes to talk about the manuscript under discussion, then make sure the Published

Writer doesn't eat up 10 minutes with her critique. When she jumps in to add her expertise to what everyone else says, request comments from all the other members as well – by name, if they refuse to open up on their own. As much as possible, ensure that the group members recognize that their opinions are also valuable and worth expressing.

I met a good friend of mine when I worked at a local bookstore. He came in to check on the sales of his novel, and I jumped at the opportunity to have a local author speak to my writing group. He agreed. The group members were thrilled to have this published author attend, and several of the members foisted their manuscripts upon him to read and evaluate. What made this man so much more than a mere Published Writer, however, was his willingness to learn from us as much as he was willing to teach us. I've often joked with him that we held him in great awe when he first attended – but as the years went by and he brought manuscripts to us for review, we developed the attitude of, "Oh, that's just him. Yes, he's been published, and he has some great things to say, but I don't always agree with him."

That's the mark of a healthy group's response to *any published author*. Yes, his opinions mattered, perhaps a bit more because he had been published, but the act of publishing didn't make him perfect, and the other members soon learned they had as much to share with him as he with us. The Published Writer hasn't learned that. She believes that the simple act of being published has bestowed upon her the crown of knowledge, and she proudly displays it every chance she gets. She may someday take critiques and learn from them, but the road to that day will be long, difficult, and probably full of disappointment (possibly even heartache as she watches her manuscripts ripped to shreds by the paid critics as well as by the Amazon masses).

A Freeloader: The Specialist

I've only run into a handful of variations of this Freeloader in all the years I've attended and led writing groups. The Specialist tends not to stay with writing groups very long, partly because he sees no value in the groups and partly because the groups react so negatively to him. As his name implies, the Specialist specializes in a particular topic or field of study.

As far as the Specialist is concerned, no one knows his topic even half as well as he knows it. He's conducted the research, he's been to the sacred sites, he's talked to the experts – he has become the expert on this particular topic. Because of this wealth of knowledge, the Specialist sees himself as a special class of person. He is part of this topic's elite, part of a group of people who comprehend this topic better than anyone else even comes close to understanding it.

When the Specialist writes his manuscripts, he knows that he's transferring some of that wealth of knowledge to his reader. However, his reader will never know as much about this topic as he knows, and the Specialist never forgets that distinction. He also never lets the reader (or the rest of the writing group) forget that distinction.

When the Specialist submits his manuscript for editing by a writing group, he really does not want to be edited. He wants the group to marvel at the depth of his knowledge. He wants to bask in praise for how many things he knows that the writing group members do not.

Let me give you an example: Several years ago, I led a writing group when a visiting Specialist dropped by to see what we were about. Our policy was for writers to distribute copies of their work, the members would take those copies home and edit them, and we would return two weeks later to discuss our critiques. This particular Specialist did not want to do things our way, though – and that was our first warning sign. You see, he was a poet, and poetry had to be read aloud to be fully expressed. Not only was he a poet, however, but he was a poet who wrote about "the Native American experience," and that experience could not be read silently at all. It had to be heard so the audience could experience the full impact of the pain that was the modern, Native American life.

We politely agreed to hear this man's poetry and critique it on the spot. (I was younger then, and much more tolerant of frivolities such as this. Anymore, I would probably tell this man we had a schedule to keep and that he should come back next time with copies of his work to distribute for proper editing.) He read his poetry, and I don't remember a single thing about it. Good or bad, I cannot say. I doubt it was awful, or I would have some memory of cringing at his reading. I also doubt it was excellent since I don't remember feeling overwhelmed by the poetry's power.

We applauded him, though, and commended the parts of his poetry that we most enjoyed. (That's one of the things I require of the groups I lead – the members must praise the good parts before they criticize anything.) When we started making suggestions to improve the work, however, this man stopped listening and started arguing with us. His first argument was that we were not poets and could not properly understand the poetic form. While I've said that about myself several times over the years, we had other members in our group who wrote, published, and won awards for their poetry, so his argument was weak at best.

His second argument was that he had written Native American poetry that expressed the Native American experience from a uniquely Native American perspective that could only be understood by Native Americans – so no wonder we didn't understand it. Since I know you're asking yourself the best question at this point: No, this man was not Native American, freely admitting that during our discussion. He was, however, a self-appointed Specialist on the topic of Native Americans. He had researched his topic until he believed he knew everything there was to know about it, and he was taking the time to share that knowledge with us through his poetry. The fact that we did not immediately acknowledge his expertise only confirmed to him that we were not yet ready to receive it. He never returned.

That is a common pattern with the Specialists I've encountered throughout the years. One Specialist was writing a marriage book. Another, a book on Islam. Someone else was writing a war novel. The thing all of those Specialists had in common was they believed themselves to be THE experts on their topics, and they did not want to hear anything critical of whatever they'd written. They attended long enough to share their work, possibly two meetings at the most, and they were never seen again.

To be fair, many Specialists have done quite a bit of research and know their topics well. They often have a passion for what they're writing, and they legitimately want to express themselves to as wide an audience as possible.

The fact of his own expertise, however, makes the Specialist unable to accept criticism of his work. He's spent so much time researching his material and becoming on expert on his topic that he interprets any criticism of the writing as a criticism of the content. He's far too sensitive (and probably too immature of a writer) to take editing as the constructive criticism that it is. He also makes the mistake of assuming that the people in the group always know less about the topic than he knows. I've been surprised several times at group members I've known for years suddenly expounding on topics I had no idea they knew.

The Specialist does very little long-term damage to a writing group, mostly because he leaves after his first couple meetings. In those meetings, however, he can be a frustrating and disruptive element to the normal flow. As my example showed, the Specialist can have little regard for the way the group usually operates. Since he doesn't anticipate attending many meetings, the Specialist wants to wring as much personal assistance (or praise) as he can from the meeting(s) he attends. He's likely to want to break the flow of a normal meeting to do things his way, either so he can leave early or so he does not have to return to the next meeting – or both. Expect the Specialist to want to distribute his material or read it aloud right there and to want immediate feedback, whether the writing group operates that way or not. If he did not bring any copies of his work with him, expect him to want to distribute his manuscript via email, possibly even collecting member's email addresses himself so that he can be sure to forward his work to them when he gets home – again, whether the writing group operates that way or not.

He might accept manuscripts from the other group members, but he won't do much editing on them or say much about them at the following meetings. That is because he either will not read them (he was too busy with his own writing and research), or because the manuscripts he receives are not within his area of specialty and he feels he has no authority upon which to judge them. (You should know how to recognize an excuse by this point in the book.) Anyone who reads has some opinion about the books he picks up. Even I – a definite non-poet – have an opinion about the poetry I read. I know what I like, and I'm enough of a writer to be able to explain what I don't like. The fact that the Specialist doesn't do even that much demonstrates that he's too self-absorbed in his own specialty to be of any long-term value to the group.

The Specialist should be easy to spot from the description I've already provided: He'll want the meeting to run his way to accommodate his schedule; he'll want his work critiqued immediately, whether that's the way the group normally operates or not; even if the group is unwilling to critique his work, he'll want to share his research at great length with anyone who will listen, often taking up great swaths of time as he recites minute details; he'll gladly accept all the praise the group has to offer regarding his manuscript or his research, but when the group offers suggestions to improve his work, he'll retaliate with semi-personal attacks on the legitimacy of the group's critiquing authority and/or he'll rebuff every suggestion and never return.

There are several things a group should do when confronted by a Specialist. First, hope that the Specialist does not attend many meetings. That may sound cruel, but the Specialist contributes little to a writing group and is often so disruptive to the group's normal flow that the best thing for everyone involved is for him to stop attending. I'm not recommending that the group force him out, though, because even a Specialist can reform and become a productive member of a good group, even a good Mentor. But I'm also not recommending that the group beg him to stay if he decides to leave.

If the Specialist decides to attend, then the group's leadership must stress the importance of the rules that have already been established. The Specialist should not be allowed to dictate to the rest of the group how or when he will distribute his work for critique. If the members read their stories aloud, then he should too; if the members are required to bring copies of their manuscript for distribution, then he should do that. If the Specialist does not want to abide by whatever rules the group has already established, then he should not be allowed to distribute his work for editing. Remember, the Specialist is one of the most self-absorbed Freeloaders you're likely to meet. His mind is focused on his research and the manuscript he can bring to the world, and he'll want things to run his way. If you let him dictate his agenda to the rest of the group, you'll soon find that he is the group. When that happens, either the group will run the way he wants it to run (with little regard for anyone else's opinions), or the other group members will stop attending and the group will slowly die – or both will happen, in that order.

Assuming you convince the Specialist to abide by the group's rules of conduct, you must still work with him to participate in a constructive manner. The Specialist is very much like a child at Christmas – he's very excited about what he's getting, but he really doesn't care whether he gives anything to anyone else. Expect him to engage with everyone while his work is critiqued, and expect that he'll sit back, slightly bored, while anyone else's manuscript is critiqued. He may even try to leave after the group finishes with his manuscript.

The Specialist must learn the value of the editing process, not only what he gains by having his own work edited but what he gains by editing other people's manuscripts. It's easy to spot the mistakes other people make, but it's much more difficult for a writer to see his own mistakes – even the blatant wons. (Whoops! Now how did I miss that misspelled word?) I've known writers who use every possible method to catch their mistakes, including reading the manuscript backwards, stuffing the manuscript in a drawer for a week and then editing it, or printing out each sentence on its own line on the page. Those are all gimmicks, though, for a process that is best learned through practice, and the Specialist is only harming himself when he refuses to practice editing techniques every chance he has.

To counteract the Specialist's reluctance, you must counteract his various arguments. First, he's likely to say that the manuscripts he critiques are all different genres than whatever he's writing/reading. As such, he does not believe he has anything valuable to add. As I said earlier, this is just an excuse. Every reader has an opinion about whatever he reads, and the Specialist has one too. His reluctance to voice his opinion is more likely based on a combination of attitudes, including his opinion that no genre other than his own is worth reading, that the forms are so different between his specialized work and anyone else's that his thoughts are irrelevant, or that he just doesn't like any other genre than his chosen one.

As to his attitude that "no other genre is worth reading," that idea is far too narrow-minded, and it's detrimental to the Specialist's own work. I grew up reading nothing but science fiction (specifically, science fiction movie books, such as Star Trek). As far as I was concerned, there was no other form worth my time. Because of the various writing groups I've attended and led, however, I've read poems, histories, theologies, mysteries, family sagas, romances, fantasies, horrors, westerns – the list goes on! All of that reading has breathed so much more depth into my writing that I look back with embarrassment on my earliest works. I was writing a caricature of one genre because I didn't know anything else, and I didn't even see the depth that my own chosen genre had to offer. Now when I write my stories, I try to incorporate some of that mystery into the plot, the romance into my characters' lives; I remember the importance of my characters' religious convictions and family histories; I acknowledge my characters' innermost fears (rational or not); and I keep in mind my space-opera genre's debt to both the 1950s westerns as well as to the ancient myths (Zeus, Aphrodite, and the gang) that I loved so much as a child.

I've heard similar stories from many of my writing-group friends. People who never gave a second thought to ever picking up a book in some other genre suddenly discover they have a story inside them that can only be told from that other genre – from that different perspective on the world. The genres are really only arbitrary divisions for separating different perspectives on the world – but the stories told within this world are never new. Consider *Dune* and *Oedipus Rex*. Both tell the story of a man moving inexorably toward his destiny, but you would never confuse one for the other. Or what about David Weber's Honor Harrington series and C.S. Forester's Horatio Hornblower series? One man rides the Earth's ocean waves while one woman rides space's gravitic waves – but they both deal with issues of love, loyalty, friendship, and what it means to be an officer in a navy. If you're still unsure, consider this: At its core, what is the story of "King Kong"? It's a romance. Don't believe me? Then you need to watch that movie again. It may appear to be a fantasy story about a giant ape terrorizing New York City, but it's really the story of a beast who falls in love with a beauty.

The Specialist, by the very act of specializing so severely on his particular field of study (or genre) will only grow as a result of his reading and editing those other forms. His time in a good writing group can help him to become a mature Mentor. It's difficult, it doesn't always turn out successfully, and the time it takes to reach that point may be frustrating for the Specialist as well as the other group members, but the end result will be worth the effort.

A Freeloader: The College Professor (Hyde)

Think back over every bad memory you have from every English teacher you've ever had going all the way back to first grade (maybe even kindergarten), throw them all into one big pot, and the resulting soup is this particular Freeloader, the College Professor.

Where the Dr. Jekyll side of the College Professor (from Chapter 3) is patient, an excellent line-editor, and an inspiration to fellow writers, the Mr. Hyde side is impatient (even irritable), condescending, and more likely to tell her fellow writers to just give up on the whole writing venture than she is to give them any constructive advice. This College Professor is as brilliant as her Dr. Jekyll alter ego, but she's intolerant of anyone who does not measure up to her exacting standards.

Of all the Freeloaders, this College Professor can be the most destructive, especially to a young writer working on her first manuscript. You see, the College Professor is jaded. She's spent her entire life trying each semester to lift mediocre writing from the abysmal pit only to have to start all over again in the following semester with an equally inept group of students, and she's decided the entire venture is nothing but endless punishment. She sees herself as a modern-day Sisyphus, that sly founder of ancient Corinth who, as punishment for binding the god of death, eternally rolled a giant boulder to the tip of the mountain – only to watch in despair as it bounced back down to the base and he had to start all over again. Her talented – but lazy, uncaring, listless – students are the boulders she struggles to lift from the depths of mediocrity; her sacred mountain is the form and rules of the English language; and her endless cycle of pushing/falling/pushing/falling is academia's semester system in which she's forever trapped, her own personal punishment for daring to believe in an ideal called "education" when she was young and naïve.

So, she joins a writing group to pursue her own dream of writing the Great American Novel, and she finds nothing more than the same kinds of uneducated students she deals with every day – except most of these people left school long ago and should know better by now. Some final straw snaps inside of her, and instead of pushing these fellow writers to excel as she pushes her students every day, she instead takes it upon herself to purge the English Literature landscape of deadwood such as these so-called writers. She eagerly accepts every manuscript distributed, and – with blood-red pen in hand – she slices and dices with fanatical precision. No misplaced pronoun or dangling modifier escapes her attention, and she's equally harsh on minor spelling offenses as she is on major grammatical errors.

The writer on the receiving end of this tirade feels as if she's dying in the shower scene of Alfred Hitchcock's "Psycho," the knife blade mercilessly slicing away at her body. No writing is ever good enough for the College Professor, and pity on the writer who dares submit such shoddy work.

The Hyde side of the College Professor can destroy both an individual writer as well as an entire writing group. The individual writer receives bleeding manuscripts with critical comments giving her such unhelpful advice as, "English is obviously not your primary language" or "Do not make another writing attempt until you have at least mastered the basics." While those kinds of remarks make the College Professor feel warm and tingly inside, they destroy a writer's sense of self-worth. No longer is the discussion about the writing and how to improve it; the discussion has turned to biting comments regarding the writer's education and command of the English language (or lack thereof).

Before I get much further, however, I need to stress that English usage rules are definitely important to a writer. A good plot will only take a story so far before clunky sentences and misspelled words make it unreadable, and in this modern age of grammar-checks and spell-checks fully installed on every app, there's little excuse for getting those elements wrong. In fact, some justification may exist for the College Professor's frustration with the manuscripts she reads. While that does not justify her thoughtless remarks during editing, it should provide some insight into the way she thinks.

All of this griping and slashing and hacking from the College Professor forces writers to believe they really don't have what it takes to write. Writers stop attending the writing group, keyboards stop clacking at

THE SUCCESSFUL WRITING GROUP

home, and stories stop swirling through people's imaginations. These broken husks return to their day jobs, more certain than ever that their aspirations of writing and publishing were pipedreams at best, and the College Professor leans back in her ivory-tower office, secure in the satisfying knowledge that she has done her duty to protect the literary landscape.

This entire example may seem like a case of the mother telling her child that she can't go out to play in the rain because she'd catch pneumonia, run up a huge hospital bill, linger a few months, and then die – in short, it may sound like one huge exaggeration. Consider, however, that many writers call their manuscripts their "babies." Even the writers who don't use such endearing terms still display great sensitivity to their work. It may not be a literal baby, but that manuscript is much more than a jumble of words on paper. It's a living, breathing extension of the writer – a part of her own soul. When the College Professor slashes that manuscript – that part of the writer's soul – her attack is felt straight in the writer's gut. While the wound may not be visible, it certainly cuts deep.

Writers can easily be crushed by this merciless onslaught, and an entire writing group can disappear within months, maybe even weeks, of the College Professor first attending. People don't like to be around mean people, and if the writing group is overrun by a Mr. Hyde, then people will simply stop attending. At that point, the group dies.

Direct intervention may be necessary to stop the College Professor before it's too late. When she makes verbal comments that aim at the writer instead of the writing, stop her and explain to her that such comments are inappropriate. If she continues, take her aside and inform her that she must stop or she will not be allowed to continue editing.

At the same time, pay special attention to the College Professor's written comments. Sometimes her spoken comments will be sugary sweet, especially in the company of writers she considers worthy of her time, but her written comments will display her caustic attitude. It may even be necessary to compare the comments on one manuscript to another, comparing what she says to a writer whose work she enjoys against what she says to a writer whose work she dislikes.

If the College Professor refuses to modify the way she critiques, the group should consider asking her to leave. That will be a tough decision to make, and it will be best for everyone involved in the group's leadership to come to agreement on this course of action first. The best thing about this is that the College Professor might leave on her own before the situation reaches this critical stage. When she sees that the writing group will not tolerate her aggressive criticism, she'll most likely leave, proclaiming to all who will listen that the group is overly tolerant of mediocrity. While I've known several of the good College Professors, I've also come across a few of the bad ones over the years, and that is the pattern they follow.

As difficult as it may be to believe, it is possible for a writer to learn something from this College Professor. She's as brilliant as her Mentor counterpart (the Dr. Jekyll College Professor from Chapter 3), and if a writer is capable of distancing herself from the vindictiveness of the remarks, the Mr. Hyde College Professor often hits on areas that really could use improvement. Whether it's worth the effort is a decision that each writer must make on her own.

Reforming the Freeloader

I've mentioned several ways that each individual Freeloader may be reformed. Be aware, however, that not every Freeloader can be reformed. Some will refuse, while others won't even realize they need reformation. Some Freeloaders believe that any problems stem entirely from the other writer(s); others just don't care, adopting the attitude that they've done their duty, and any negative consequences are someone else's responsibility.

Assuming your Freeloader is of the passive variety (Chapter 4), reformation is not only possible but quite likely. The Storyteller, the Cheerleader, and the Sponge are, at their cores, relatively benign. While they don't contribute much substantial to a writing group, especially when they first begin attending, they also do not actively try to harm the group or its members. Reforming a passive Freeloader is more a matter of training him in the group's methods and expectations. The Storyteller wants to digress at every opportunity; don't let him. Keep him on task. The Cheerleader (in many ways a mirror opposite of the bad College Professor) doesn't want to say anything negative about anyone's efforts. He has to learn the value of a constructive criticism, something that goes beyond mere silence or a half-hearted "I liked it." The Sponge doesn't feel he has anything worth contributing. He sits silently, absorbing the comments and discussions swirling around him, all the time telling himself that the group is better off not bothering with his naïve questions or opinions. What he fails to realize, though, is that his questions have been asked before, will be asked again, and are probably being asked by someone else at the table at that very moment who is also too shy to speak up. The entire group will benefit when the Sponge finally speaks, voicing either a question or a comment. Either will add tremendously to the group's discussion because the Sponge already soaked up so much information that both his questions and his comments are insightful.

The active Freeloaders (Chapter 5) are often a much bigger problem. The Egotist, the Nit-Picker, the Student of Writing, the Published Writer, the Specialist – they all believe they're acting in the best interests of the writer. Even the College Professor, when he pushes out a young, "untalented" writer, believes that he's acting in the best interest of the writing profession as a whole. Those Freeloaders are much harder to counteract because of this belief in their own benevolence. They must first be shown that their actions are harming their fellow writers (or, as with the bad College Professor, they must be forced to *care* that their actions are harming others), and then they must reform their actions to be truly beneficial. That is not an easy task.

Some of those Freeloaders can be reformed with time and simple persistence. Remind the Nit-Picker that he cannot spend five minutes enumerating every misplaced comma. Encourage the Student of Writing to actually finish his latest novel instead of endlessly revising those first 20 pages. Stop the Specialist (subtly if you can, blatantly if you must) before he completely disrupts the meeting's normal flow.

Other Freeloaders will resist the group's best efforts at reformation. The Egotist knows that his writing is better than everyone else's, and he sees no reason to change the way he writes or critiques. The Published Writer already achieved his goal of published fame and notoriety, and as long as the editors and agents keep calling him, he will never believe he has anything to learn from the unpublished masses. The College Professor, brilliant as he is, wants nothing more than to purge the dead-wood that's damming the literary stream. To encourage the untalented writers to keep writing is contrary to the bad College Professor's entire goal of literary purity.

With those kinds of Freeloaders, the writing group members (especially the leaders) must work extra hard. Start with a written set of rules that everyone follows at all meetings, written guidelines that the members adhere to when critiquing, and a strictly enforced format that the members use to discuss manuscripts. Encourage each member of the group to participate equally. Do not let any one member take over the entire critiquing session. Encourage both the published and the unpublished to voice their opinions and questions, and never let any writer attack another writer. The writing group is for the mutual benefit of all its members, and personal attacks (or even attacks on another person's writing abilities) are counterproductive and damaging to everyone's ability to effectively write and critique.

One other factor to keep in mind when considering the reformation of Freeloaders is that they may not be around long enough to be reformed. While the passive Freeloaders usually want to improve both their own writing and that of their fellow writers, the active Freeloaders can be more selfish. As a general rule, their own writing comes first, second, and third. The writing produced by others is only important so far as it can be compared to the Freeloader's own work – and while that comparison is in the Freeloaders favor, he is happy. (Well, maybe not "happy," but he's at least content.)

When other members show signs of improvement or signs of listening to somebody other than the Freeloader – when the Freeloader's absolute authority and unequaled skill is questioned – then the Freeloader has little reason to attend the group. To the Egotist, the group has lost its focus (him); to the Nit-Picker, the group isn't spending nearly enough time on the "essentials" of writing; to the Student of Writing, the other writers are doing everything wrong; to the Published Writer, no one is willing to listen to the voice of experience; to the Specialist, there are too many conflicting points of view to really learn anything useful; and to the College Professor, the writing group is merely hastening the destruction of Western literature.

When the Freeloaders express those kinds of attitudes, they won't be around much longer. They may simply stop attending, or they might tell the leader how unproductive the group is. As much like a B-Hollywood flick as it sounds, some Freeloaders will even make a stirring proclamation during a meeting, voicing their displeasure regarding the group's lack of ability. (Remember the Specialist who wrote Native American poetry? He was one such person who proudly proclaimed how little our opinions meant to him – and then we never saw him again.)

Work with those active Freeloaders as much as possible while they attend, but don't fret if (or when) they disappear. Give them the same encouragement and constructive criticism you give everyone else because you never know which ones are open to reform, are open to growing into real Mentors. Remember, we're always looking to encourage and improve both writers and writing groups.

Reforming Yourself – Yikes!

It's possible as you've been reading these chapters that you've recognized yourself among some of the various Freeloaders. If that's happened, don't freak out. Introspection is wonderful, and the ability to change is one of the best things about being human.

First, understand that I use the term "Freeloader" because that's what some people do with writing groups; they take good stuff from the other attendees, but they do not give good stuff back. They are benefiting from others without providing benefit in return. As such, if you see yourself in any of these descriptions start with one simple question: "What can I give to my fellow writers?"

For example, consider my description of the Sponge, that person who attends the group, listens to everything everyone says, but never speaks up on her own. It's possible you're shy, introverted, or uncomfortable in social situations, and those are all understandable reasons for not speaking up. However, once you ask yourself the question, "What can I give to my fellow writers?" through the lens of my overriding principle, "Be kind," you should see that the simplest, quickest, easiest comment to make is one of encouragement. Tell the author what you liked and why you liked it. You've immediately begun your journey toward mentoring.

As another example, consider the Nit-Picker. If you see yourself doing what I've described, such as taking time to describe why each and every comma is incorrect, then practice my recommendation: "Point out the problem and offer a helpful solution" – then immediately move on. For example, if the writer always forgets the comma in a compound sentence (a sentence with two subjects/verbs joined by a conjunction such as "and," "but," or "or"), then feel free to mark it every time you spot it, but you only have to mention it once: "I noticed you're forgetting the comma in your compound sentences. Be sure to put those in." As I said previously, the Nit-Picker usually has excellent points for the writer (those commas need to be in those compound sentences), but it's the way in which he points out the errors that becomes problematic to the group's functioning.

So, if you see yourself in these descriptions, that's wonderful. Look back on my chapter of Mentors, find someone you would most like to emulate, and practice the techniques I've described. You might be surprised how quickly you partner with your fellow writers, assisting and encouraging each other to grow beyond your wildest expectations.

6

Location, Location, Location...

I attended and led writing groups in a variety of locations, and they all had their pros and cons. What a group must decide is whether the known good points outweigh the bad points, and the members must plan for how best to compensate for any problems that arise – and problems will always arise.

No matter how much research and planning goes into the choice of a location for the writing group, something will come up that makes that location seem like the worst choice ever. The restaurant with the great back room will decide to remodel. The library with the excellent location will change its hours. The bookstore that welcomed you two years ago gets a new manager who decides you're no longer allowed to use the tables and chairs.

When those unexpected problems pop up, they disrupt the group's sense of stability. No matter what the group does to compensate for those problems, some members won't be happy, and some may never return. The best advice is to find the best time and location that works for the most people and stay with it as long as possible. Avoid unnecessary changes, and do not make changes based on the latest whim. Stability is one of the writing group's best assets. If people know when and where to find the group, they will attend.

The following are five locations I've used throughout the years and my experiences with each. Some of these locations were my choice, and others were in place when I began attending a group. I'll tell you about the great ones as well as the ones that never worked for us – and why. Use the following discussions as guidelines, advice to help your writing group make the most of the time and location you choose and to avoid the worst mistakes that I made over the years.

Homes

Opening a home to the writing group seems like a natural idea. After all, we write in our homes. Why not also meet there with other writers?

A house can be a good location for several reasons. First, the writing group doesn't have to worry about weird store hours or a restaurant that requires everyone to eat a meal in exchange for a table or backroom space. Barring family vacations and children's bedtimes, a home can be the most widely available space for meetings at any time of the day or night.

A home can also be quiet and comfortable, conducive to reading, editing, and critiquing. I've attended in-home meetings that met in the kitchen, at a dining room table, or in the living room on sofas and chairs, and I found them all to be relaxed and inviting atmospheres.

Someone's home can also be a much less expensive location to hold meetings. Instead of room-rental fees and overpriced meals, group members can pool their resources for coffee and cookies. That kind of group effort also brings the members closer together. They learn each other's tastes – such as the fact that I don't like coffee. They begin to know each other on a level that goes beyond their own writing, and that is healthy for a group. When the members truly know and care for each other, they often produce better critiques. It's no longer a matter of expressing an opinion; it's now become an act of helping a friend improve her work, a much more personal endeavor.

There are negative points to meeting in someone's home, too. First – and most important – hosting a writing group is time-consuming, and it can soon become a chore instead of a joy. What may seem like a fun adventure the first couple times a group meets in someone's home can become a burden on both her and her family as the weeks and months go by. Even when people bring their own snacks and drinks, and even when the members stay after the meeting to help clean up, the entire enterprise can begin to feel overwhelming.

Rotating the location from one member's house to another for each meeting may seem like a good alternative, but that often results in confusion and miscommunication among members. There always seems to be one member who forgets where the meeting's being held this month. Shifting locations also makes it difficult to consistently advertise the group's meeting time and location in community bulletin boards, calendars, or online, and a visitor who catches only one announcement may not realize that the next month's meeting (when she finally has the time to attend) will be held somewhere else.

Someone's home can also be an intimidating location for a visitor. Think about it from her perspective: She's a shy writer who spends most of her time sitting in a dim office and staring at a computer screen. She works with words from her own imagination as Dean Martin plays on her headphones, and she takes occasional breaks to sip hot chocolate and play with the cat. She has her routine, she has her comfort zone, and she's content. She hears about a writing group, and she's intrigued by the idea. But the group meets in someone's home – the home of another writer, in fact. Someone who might listen to Metallica or who drinks mint tea or who owns a dog. How is she expected to feel comfortable in someone else's writing environment when it's so different from her own?

Overall, meeting in someone's home can work well as long as the group is content with the number of people already attending. It can be an intimidating atmosphere for a visitor, and it can make advertising and promotion more difficult. Those problems can be overcome with a little creativity, though, and the relief from not worrying about store or library hours and regulations is welcome to most groups.

Restaurants

I've been involved in several groups that met in restaurants, and the results were mixed. Much of the success of meeting at a restaurant depends on the time, the day, and the popularity of the restaurant where the group meets. Obviously, the crowd is smaller if the group meets outside of a standard mealtime. On the other hand, some restaurants are only open during mealtimes. The group will have an easier time reading and critiquing if it can meet in a back room, but many restaurants don't have back rooms – or if they do, they might charge a room rental fee. Most restaurants are also structured around the principle that patrons come in quickly, eat quickly, and leave quickly so that the table can be cleared for the next group of patrons who will come in quickly, eat quickly, etc. (If you doubt this, try spending a couple hours at a busy restaurant. You'll soon discover that your drink glasses remain empty and the server repeatedly asks if you'd prefer to pay with check or credit card. If it's a particularly snobby restaurant, you may even receive glares from the employees.)

If you're willing to work around those problems, though, a restaurant can be a good location for a writing group meeting. Unlike someone's home, a restaurant is neutral ground, a place where everyone feels both comfortable and yet slightly out of place. At once it can belong to both everyone and to no one – assuming it's a restaurant that everyone agrees upon. Most restaurants play bland music at a low enough volume that it can be ignored, and if you choose someplace with a wide variety of food, most people will find something to eat or drink.

Restaurants also offer the group a well-known, stable location that can be easily used in advertising and public service announcements; they usually have their own parking lots with plenty of space; and especially during off hours, they usually appreciate the extra, repeat business and good publicity that a group brings.

Some restaurants have back rooms or sections of the dining room that they make available for group meetings, and those rooms can often be reserved – for a price. Private rooms provide the group with a quieter, more private space to hold meetings, but a cordoned-off portion of the dining room gives the group a greater exposure. I'm often surprised by how many people start attending a writing group after "eavesdropping" in one of those public locations.

A restaurant is not without its drawbacks, of course. Primarily, restaurants are not natural fits for writing groups. As I said, a restaurant's purpose is to feed people as quickly as possible and make room for the next group of hungry people. While a restaurant may be more welcoming to a group meeting during a slower time of the day, and while a back room may exist for just such meetings, restaurants are still focused on the business of feeding people. If the group members don't eat, the restaurant probably won't see the point in hosting them. Even if the members eat, the restaurant may insist on a room rental fee above the cost of the food and drinks.

Overall, a restaurant can be a good location for group meetings, as long as you find a place where most people enjoy the food. (As much as I enjoy Thai food, I probably wouldn't host a meeting in a Thai restaurant because most people don't consider it "average American" food. In that type of situation, bland variety is probably the safest bet.) If your group members can afford the cost of food and drinks and possibly a room rental fee, then a restaurant might work.

Bookstores

Writers and bookstores and books! They all go together, and the writing group is a natural fit in that mix. The most successful writing group I ever led met in a Barnes & Noble for nearly a decade. When that store no longer agreed to host us, a local Waldenbooks agreed to sponsor our group. (Remember Waldenbooks? I really miss those mall bookstores.) While the Waldenbooks was too small to host meetings, they agreed to promote the group and help set up speaking engagements with authors, editors, and agents. In short, a good relationship with a bookstore can benefit both the store and the writing group.

The first thing to decide is what the group needs from the bookstore, because not all bookstores can offer a place to meet. Mall-based stores, if you can still find one, do not have the space to host a writing group, and many independent bookstores barely have room for the books on the shelves, a cash register by the door, and the coffee bar along the windows. A Books-a-Million or a Barnes & Noble may have space available, but that space often disappears during the busy Thanksgiving and Christmas holidays. On the other hand, my B&N writing group did quite well meeting January through November, so even an abbreviated year can work.

There are several good and bad things you can expect from a large, chain bookstore that agrees to host a writing group. Besides the guaranteed space each month, most chain bookstores do quite a bit of advertising for their sponsored events. Many bookstores post a calendar of events on which they'll list the group's meeting time, and some send their employees to local radio stations to discuss upcoming events, while others send their events lists to cable franchises and social media.

As well as the media exposure, the writing group will also get quite a bit of advertising just from meeting in such a public place. Writers frequent bookstores, and many writers are guilty of eavesdropping (or "conducting research" as I prefer to call it). I've watched other "researching writers" hover on the edge of a meeting, pretending to be engrossed in some book as they surreptitiously glance our way, sometimes smiling at a joke or nodding at a well-spoken opinion on some writing technique. That is the best advertising your group could hope for: you're presenting your message *directly* to a potential member, you're reaching an audience that is *interested*, and you're doing so in an environment that feels *safe*.

Problems can, of course, arise when working with a chain bookstore. I was starting a new group in North Dakota, and I scheduled a 7 p.m. time with a chain bookstore. The store put us in the coffee shop, which had ample space for us, but we had difficulty reading and critiquing over the constant noise of the cappuccino machine. As if that wasn't difficult enough, however, the store had also scheduled an 8 p.m. brass band to play Christmas carols – in that same coffee shop. Editing came to a halt when we couldn't hear each other above the trumpets merrily tooting the Christmas cheer.

Chain bookstores also have quite a bit of employee turnover, including the management team. One chain store I worked with went through three community relations managers in only two years. As I said, the most successful writing group I led met in a Barnes & Noble for almost a decade, but when the management team at that store changed over, the new store manager decided he didn't want to host groups like ours anymore. New employees have different ideas on how the store should operate, and that can have a huge impact on a writing group that uses that space for meetings. Not only that, but chain stores are supervised by district and regional managers who tell the stores how to operate to fit a corporate norm. One chain store refused to list our writing group in the monthly calendar because the district manager didn't like writing groups – and the store manager hadn't even told him about us! It wasn't until that district manager went elsewhere that the store began advertising our group.

Writing groups can also develop good relationships with smaller chain bookstores and independent bookstores, even when the stores are too small to host group meetings. Bookstore owners and managers attend conferences and meetings across the country, and they often meet editors, agents, and authors at those meetings. A well-connected manager may be able to invite special speakers that writing group members would never be able to contact on their own. If the special speaker is an author with a recently-published book, the store can host her for a signing and reading while the writing group hosts her as a special speaker. The publicity from such an event will help everyone involved: the author gets publicity for her new book, the writing group gets a well-known speaker, and the store sells a few more books.

One of the biggest problems with a small, chain store is that the group may still need a place to actually meet. Chain stores may see little value in the effort of supporting a writing group when their corporate offices require them to promote certain sales events and authors at different times of the year anyway. Independent bookstores may be more open to the relationship, but the group may still need a larger location in which to meet.

Libraries and Community Centers

Libraries and community centers are very good places to hold writing group meetings. The locations are well known, they're public, and they're often advertised. Unlike homes, these locations are neutral, places where visitors will feel comfortable just dropping by. Rooms in libraries and community centers are often free (or available for a very small fee), and they may even be stocked with a coffeemaker or a vending machine for snacks and drinks.

I've found three problems with using rooms in libraries, though. They're often booked months in advance, the library may restrict the number of times a group can use a room, and the library's hours may not be convenient for a group to meet. For example, one library I contacted for a meeting had only one room available. We booked it, and then discovered that this last remaining room was in the cold, dark basement, far away from any other people – and even a little scary! Another library we contacted would only allow our group to meet once a month. That didn't work because our group was so large we were barely getting all our work done while holding two meetings each month.

Community center rooms often have the same kinds of pros and cons. They're centrally located, visible, advertised, and welcoming to visitors. On the other hand, the rooms may only be available for a fee, the group may get the last room available, and the hours may not work for the group members.

Location, Location, Location...

This discussion of location comes down to what works best for your group. I've met in all five of the above locations, and I have my personal favorites. However, I'd set aside my own preferences if it meant getting more people to attend the meetings. The two biggest factors for a group's success are consistency and advertising. Of those two, however, consistency is the more important. You can promote your group through emails, fliers, social media, or even paid advertising on radio or television, but if the group meets in a new location each month, people won't know where to find it.

That isn't to say that a group should meet in one location forever. I attended a writing group that was slowly dying as members just stopped attending and those who remained never wrote anything. (Or if they did, they never brought their work to the meetings.) The group met in a community center that charged an exorbitant fee for the small space we used, and the yearly dues to maintain the room were discouraging. (I deal more with charging dues in Chapter 7.) We needed a change of location, but the leadership at the time was unwilling to make the change. The meetings weren't helping my writing, and I was leading another group that was quite active, so I simply stopped attending. Within a year, that group, which had existed for nearly 50 years, disappeared completely. While a change in location may have only postponed the inevitable, it might also have breathed new life into such a stagnating group.

A group should remain consistent until such time as a change becomes necessary. When that happens, though, the group's leadership must be willing to embrace the change and make it as positive an influence on the group as possible. To conclude this chapter, the following paragraphs are two examples of times when my group needed to make a change and how we dealt with it.

One group I led had been growing steadily. We started with about four people (counting me and my wife) at each meeting, and we had grown to an average of about 12 within two years. However, we had as many as 14 or 15 on nights when visitors dropped by. That made for longer meetings where we had more trouble getting through all the material, and several members suggested that we split our one group into two smaller groups. As the leader, it was my decision, and I was unwilling to make that change. While our highs could hit 15, our lows could still get down to six. I worried that five people might attend one group while only one person attended the other.

I resisted for nearly six months the calls to split up the group, but then one night we had a full house – every one of our members attended. Suddenly, with no visitors at all, we had reached a new high of 16 people at a single meeting, and I could not keep everyone focused on the task of editing and critiquing. While one side of the table discussed the manuscript at hand, the other side of the table (that had already voiced their comments) broke down into whispered conversations of other manuscripts and project ideas. By the time I quieted the whispers on that side of the table, the other side had moved on to the next manuscript without me realizing it. I discovered that night just how difficult it was to wrangle 16 distractible writers onto the same topic at the same time, and I decided the group needed to be split in half.

I did not make the change arbitrarily, though. I emailed three people who had attended the group for years, people I considered leadership in the group even though they did not lead the group. I valued their opinions, and I knew they would give me good advice as I made this major change. I also did not share my plans with anyone else in the group. While I knew that several other people might offer wonderful suggestions, I did not want to open the discussion to every opinion that might delay the entire process. (We had tried to come up with a name for our group some time earlier, and it took us nearly a year to all agree on that decision! I did not want to take another year deciding who would go into which group.)

As the group's leader, I made the big decisions myself. (That's the first thing a group leader must realize. As leader, I was responsible for whatever final decisions were made, so I made them and moved on.) I listed all the members on a sheet of paper, listed the strengths and weaknesses that I saw in each of them, and divided them up as I thought best so that each person's strength complemented another person's weakness. My goal was to create two groups that were as balanced as possible so that no one would feel cheated out of a critique he really wanted.

The result was a success. Each group not only survived on its own but thrived quite well. We divided visitors between us, we allowed people to switch groups if they asked, and we continued to grow, hitting highs in the low 20s within another two years.

Another time I had to make a major change to one of my groups, the change was forced upon us. As I said earlier, one of my writing groups met in a chain bookstore for several years. The store management changed, though, and the new management team decided they no longer wanted to host any groups at all – not book groups, poetry groups, or writing groups.

It would have been easy for us to get resentful and bitter toward the store and the managers, but we approached the situation as an opportunity for our group to grow in new directions. As if the change in location wasn't hard enough on our group, I was preparing to move across the country, and I had just turned over the leadership of the group to another member. We looked into all of the locations I discussed earlier in this chapter, including a couple I didn't mention, such as an empty store in the local mall. We considered our current location, the chain bookstore, and the limitations it placed on our group, and then we looked at other locations and the potential they offered for future growth and advertising.

The new leader, a wonderfully enthusiastic woman who did a great job throughout this transition, decided to move the group to a community center. The center had shorter hours, which meant the group had to meet earlier in the evening, but the center also offered tremendous growth opportunities for the group, both in increased advertising and in the amount of space available for the meetings. That group, I am thrilled to report, is still going strong more than 15 years after that transition.

Consistency is a key factor for a group to succeed, but change is sometimes necessary. The stories I've told are both examples of how change, at the right time, can be instrumental in a writing group's ongoing success. Hold the change off as long as possible, but embrace the change when it becomes necessary.

7

It's All About the Program

In this final chapter, I'll discuss the program opportunities that are available to a writing group. These include such things as parties and special speakers, but the ideas are not limited to the ones I mention. The following program opportunities are the ones I've seen or used at various times while attending and leading writing groups. Some of them worked great for us; others...not so great. Take what your group can best use and have fun. If you come up with a great, new idea, email it to me at hdean@hdeanfisher.com and let me know. I love trying new things in the groups I lead.

Special Speakers

My philosophy on special speakers is simple: they must be special.

There are two ways that special speakers are special. First, they need to have something to say that matters to the group. If everyone in the group writes fiction, and no one has any interest in non-fiction, then inviting a special speaker from the local newspaper to discuss writing news articles is a waste of time. Find special speakers who have something to say to the group, who could help improve the kinds of manuscripts the members write – or who can help your members sell their work.

At separate meetings, I invited the fantasy author James Stoddard and the mystery author D. R. Meredith to speak to one of my groups. Mr. Stoddard had just published his first fantasy novel (*The High House*) through Warner Aspect, and the sequel was due out soon. Ms. Meredith had recently released her first Reading Group Mysteries novel (*Murder in Volume*), and she was on a book-signing tour to promote the series. Both authors were great special speakers, and I'll tell you why.

First, while those two authors were traveling the region to promote their books, they did not use our group as a sales opportunity. We told them we wanted to know about the writing process and about their search for agents and publishers, and they stuck to those topics. They related their experiences and gave us tips for working in the publishing industry – without commercials.

Also, because Stoddard and Meredith published what the group members wrote (genre fiction), the authors could give the kind of advice we needed. We wanted to know about sample chapters, query letters to agents, and dealing with editors – topics the special speakers knew firsthand.

Most important, however, was that the special speakers shared their experiences freely with the group. Authors are unique in that they often relate to newer writers in an apprentice-like manner, teaching and encouraging the newer writers to accomplish great things. Unfortunately, not all special speakers have learned that role in a writing group situation. A couple years after D. R. Meredith spoke to our group, we invited another author (who shall remain nameless), and that author spent the entire time promoting her book instead of assisting the group members to become better writers.

I've had many other successes with special speakers, though. Non-fiction author Dennis Covington (*Salvation on Sand Mountain*) spoke to my Lubbock, Texas, group and drew an excellent crowd of 52 people to the bookstore that evening. A now-retired agent spoke to one of my groups, and she gave the members great advice for securing representation – and better yet, for knowing when they really needed representation. We invited book editors Kim Campbell and Karen Smith to speak, and we enjoyed their presentation on self-editing so much that we asked them back twice in the following year, once for a mini-conference on script writing and again for a refresher course on self-editing.

Special speakers can do wonderful things for a writing group, but you must keep the following things in mind:

1) Have a reason for inviting the speaker. Don't invite a special speaker just because you can. Make sure she has experience, knowledge, contacts – something! – that she can present. If she has nothing to say, then why is she saying anything?

2) If the special speaker has published books, encourage the group members to buy one and read it before she speaks. When she arrives, ask questions related to her book. That does two things: First, it conveys a respect and interest in her work that goes beyond a mere celebrity status, and second, it gives her and the group members a common frame of reference that she can use as she's speaking. Points she makes in her presentation won't be mere abstracts of thought because she can relate those points to the book everyone read. (And when she's through speaking, she can autograph everyone's copy.)

3) Promote the event. Let your local radio and television stations know who's coming to speak. Place announcements on community bulletin boards. Announce it on your social media platforms and/or website. If your special speaker is willing, line up a talk-radio or tele-vision interview. Post a video on YouTube or TikTok. You won't get visitors attending your meeting if they don't know something special is happening.

4) Treat the special speaker as an honored guest and the speaking engagement as an opportunity to celebrate. Offer her a cup of coffee or a soda. Have someone bring cookies or doughnuts for all to share. A couple times I even promoted a pre-event dinner with the speaker for group members only (no visitors), and we all pitched in to buy dinner for the speaker.

5) *Take care of the monetary arrangements early.* Some speakers charge a fee, others require people to buy their books, and some people will speak for travel/gas money only. Find out right away what a speaker charges or what she's willing to take in exchange for speaking. I've been fortunate because most of the special speakers I invited agreed to speak for free or for only gas money if they had to travel quite a distance to reach us. But I asked right away, and we agreed on the monetary arrangements before we confirmed a date.

6) *Be prepared for visitors.* If you've publicized the special speaker, you're likely to get at least a couple people dropping by, and possibly – hopefully! – many more. The largest meeting I ever led happened when 52 people heard Dennis Covington speak on the topic of creative non-fiction. We used every chair the bookstore had in the back room, and we still had people standing in the aisles. I distributed a sign-up sheet if people wanted to receive emails about our group's meeting, and I briefly explained the concept of a writing group before Covington got up to speak. A special speaker is an excellent opportunity to publicize your group to people who may have never thought about attending. Don't waste the opportunity.

With good planning and proper arrangements, a special speaker can be a great event for a writing group, both to inspire the writers and to promote the group to potential visitors. Have fun with it.

Socializing

No matter how popular the phrase, people are not just islands drifting through the sea of life. People are social. People enjoy the company of other real, physical people – not just online people. And no matter how much some writers might argue that it's not true, we are the same way. Writers need to socialize. Writers need to talk about something other than writing. ("Gasp!" you say.)

Socializing outside the group meetings is a great way for writers to get to know each other as real people instead of knowing them only as other writers. When we have the opportunity to connect on more than one level, we gain a better understanding of each other, a deeper level of respect for one another.

As much as I push my writing groups to focus on the writing, I also push my group members to socialize outside of the regular meeting times. Individually, I've met with some of my members for coffee, lunch, chit-chatty brainstorming sessions, or even for racquetball. I know I'm not alone in doing this either as I've heard stories of my writers visiting each other at home or meeting at the mall for an afternoon of shopping. While I don't personally encourage this kind of thing, I even knew two members who met at the writing group, started dating, and got married.

As a leader, I've found one way to encourage the group members to socialize is to host parties. We held summer parties and Christmas parties for several years, and they were always well attended. One person would volunteer to host the party at his/her house, and everyone else would bring the food, potluck-style. At Christmas we enjoyed white-elephant gift exchanges, and in the summer we enjoyed barbecues. If someone had recently had a manuscript published, we made her/him stand in front and read to us – and you better believe we applauded when they were done! We played games (Catch-Phrase was a favorite). Mostly, though, the parties were a chance for us to relax and socialize outside of the rigors of reading and critiquing.

As always throughout this book, however, I recommend you keep the socializing balanced with the other activities. One or two parties throughout the year always seemed to work well for me, but my groups were very serious during the meetings. We didn't allow much time for chit-chat in the middle of critiquing, so the parties were a great chance to do that. If group members spend most of their time chatting about unrelated topics, though, the leadership needs to focus on the task at hand – editing and critiquing – instead of party-planning.

Advertising

When I say advertising, I'm not talking about only those 30-second television ads. In fact, in all the years I attended or led writing groups, we never paid for any advertising – and certainly not for a 30-second television spot. Even if we could have afforded it, there are so many other ways to promote writing groups that we probably wouldn't have placed an ad on television or radio.

When you think of how to promote a writing group, think one word: free. That's likely the only advertising a writing group can afford (there is some truth to that starving-writer stereotype). On the plus side, though, free advertising forces you to think of promotional opportunities that will actually reach potential writers. For example, whereas a 30-second radio spot will cover your hometown once and reach a couple people who thought they could maybe write a book someday, a flier stuck on the wall outside your local college's English department will be seen by dozens – possibly hundreds – of people who write all the time. A glossy television ad might look really cool, but a notice posted in your local library will be seen by people with a love of reading. Put up a website, a social media page, or a MeetUp listing. Be sure to list when and where you meet; list your website; list your social media sites and handles. Since the people who love to read are often the same people who love to write, your notice will be seen by exactly the people you're trying to reach.

Let your local bookstores know that your writing group exists – and be sure to talk to your local, independent bookstores, not just the big chains. If your group doesn't actually meet inside a chain bookstore, that chain probably won't want to promote you. But independent bookstores work more intimately with their customers, promoting not only the bookstore's agenda but also events around town that the store's customers might want to attend. Keep in mind, however, that no matter how nice your independent bookstore might be, the manager probably won't promote the writing group that meets at the competitor chain store down the block.

If there's a college or university nearby, promote your writing group there. Make sure the English and journalism departments know about the group. Get permission, and then post fliers on bulletin boards and outside classrooms.

All of this is not to say that you can never use radio and television, but you should use them for a reason instead of just because they're easy. Special-speaker appearances are events designed to promote the writing group in a big way, and radio and television offer some great opportunities – again, though, think beyond the 30-second advertisement.

Many local television and talk-radio stations have morning and noon newscasts where they interview "ordinary people doing extraordinary things." By that definition, authors are often considered extraordinary people. Ask your special speaker if she'd be willing to go on television to promote her books and your writing group, and then plan to go on with her. The anchor will ask each of you to speak for a minute or two, and the station will probably flash your group's meeting time and contact information on the screen. All of that happens for free, and I've found that those kinds of programs are often eager to schedule guests. Contact the station far enough in advance, though, so the proper arrangements can be made.

Paying Dues

I've attended groups that charge annual dues and groups that do not, and I've found benefits to both. The groups that charge dues can often do very impressive things with that money. They can afford to bring in special speakers from farther away, those who might have to drive several hours or even fly to reach the meeting. They can more easily hold writing conferences, whether those are larger or smaller in scale, because they can pay for the accommodations, promotional materials, and special speakers. They can even afford cookies and coffee at the meetings.

While membership is usually inexpensive, though, it's still one more expense for people to consider each year. I've found $15-$50 per year to be about the average for group memberships, but I've also found that the money comes due at the most inconvenient time. (It doesn't matter what time of year, either. One additional bill always comes at an inconvenient time.)

Charging membership dues also puts a distinct monetary value on the work the group does. Whether you charge $5 or $100, someone will wonder, "Am I getting my money's worth?" If the answer ever becomes "No," people will stop attending – or they'll grumble and devolve into Freeloaders.

I've never charged membership dues at the writing groups I've led. I believe that people should have the freedom to come and go from the group as they choose, and the dues restricted that freedom of movement. Who am I to say that the latest visitor shouldn't benefit from our knowledge because he can't afford the yearly membership price?

However, that meant that our special speakers were often...ourselves. Not that we didn't know what we were talking about. I spoke once on character development, and another friend spoke on query letters. We knew what we were talking about, but it's harder to promote a special speaker as an event worthy of the public's attention when that event is titled "Joe, the local English teacher, discussing active-voice writing." Special speakers have a flare. There's a certain rockstar quality to them that makes them easier to promote. They are an event.

Because we didn't charge dues, we took up special collections to cover speakers' expenses. A few quick calculations usually did it: gas to and from at $2 per gallon (that was a long time ago!), assume the speaker makes 15 miles per gallon, throw in a Starbucks coffee, divide all of that by the number of people attending, and everyone owes me $5. Time to pass the hat.

Of course, I ran the risk that somebody wouldn't pay or that the people who weren't interested in the topic wouldn't show up. As the leader, I always threw in an extra few dollars so everyone saw me leading by example – but as the leader, I also caught the back end of that deal, picking up the slack from whoever did not (or could not) contribute. Where everyone else pitched in $5, I usually paid an extra $10 to $15. I thought it was worth it to help grow the group, but you have to decide how much you're willing to help – or if it's even feasible for you to do that. Sometimes, one special speaker will know another, and the second speaker may expect the same deal as the first. Don't start a pattern of throwing in a little extra money if you don't think you can continue it.

Conclusion

BALANCE

A writing group can be a fun and exciting opportunity to socialize, learn, and grow. It can also be a wasted time of non-stop chit-chatting, an aggravating time of unhelpful critiques, or a disheartening time of unwarranted personal attacks. Much depends on the people involved.

Make decisions from the beginning, and don't put them off until someone asks or complains. What do you want your writing group to be? Do you want special speakers? Do you want to pay dues? Do you want to critique aloud or take the stories home to read at your leisure?

Take a stand immediately. Will you tolerate Freeloaders? How will you encourage Mentors to attend? What will you do when someone launches a personal attack on a fellow author? Will you be able to lead by example?

Strike a balance that works for you. How often will you meet? Do you want special speakers at every meeting? Once a month? Once a year? Will you ever socialize outside of your meetings? Will you host a Christmas party? Will you host a Chinese New Year party? (Those are legitimate questions. Don't expect that everyone who attends your writing group will be of your religion or nationality.)

I've given you options throughout this book, and I've told you what worked best for me. It's up to you to decide what will work best for your group and your fellow writers.

I also warned you of the various Freeloaders I've encountered throughout the years. I told you how to spot them, what to expect from them when they attend, and I suggested ways of dealing with them. Please remember, however, that "Freeloaders" are still people. Take the high road when dealing with everyone. It may feel good to cut down people when they attack you, but two sets of hurt feelings don't improve the situation.

Thinking back to my 1979 masterpiece, "The Seventh Battle," and my mother telling me it needed some rewrites, I realize what a great Mentor she was. How easy would it have been to tell me I was brilliant, throw the book into an envelope, and pretend to mail it off for me? I was 9, and I wouldn't have known the difference. But how long would I have gone on believing my words were perfect on the first draft?

Twenty years? Thirty? Would I be willing to rewrite today if my mother had told me my writing was perfect back then?

That's the kind of Mentor a good author needs. You need a Mentor who can look at your work, honestly evaluate the strengths and weaknesses, and make suggestions to improve it. That person may be your mother, spouse, best friend, or stranger on the internet. Writing groups are great places to meet up with just such Mentors. Wherever you find them, thank your lucky stars for that person – and then return the favor in kind. Be that Mentor for someone else. You'll not only improve your writing and editing skills, but you'll have the satisfaction of knowing you helped a fellow writer grow into an excellent author.

The point remains: If you want to write a fantastic story – one that you can be proud of for years to come – don't show it to just anybody. Let a Mentor into your life and grow into a writer who not only crafts the words contained in that first (rough!) draft, but a writer who goes through the real work of editing, revising, and rewriting. In two words: be a *Mentor*, and be an *Author*.

H. Dean Fisher
Photo by John Kilker,
JohnJKilker.com

H. Dean Fisher is author of the fantastic, the scientifically fictional, and the macabre. His fiction and photography has won awards at various conferences and competitions throughout the United States. He currently teaches mass communication and writing, and his research interests include gender representation in videogame journalism; credibility in public relations and broadcasting; and mythological portrayals in media.

Website: www.hdeanfisher.com - sign up for the monthly newsletter.
Facebook: www.facebook.com/seventhbattlepublishing
Twitter: @HDeanFisher1
Instagram: HDeanFisher

"Medusa: Rise of a Goddess"
Medusa: The monster from legend, with snakes for hair and a gaze that turns humans to stone. Cursed by Athena for the crime of being raped, she was destined to be slain by Perseus. Except, she never died. The stories got it wrong.

At the dawn of creation, the girl Medusa lives with her family on the Eastern Edge of the World, but she yearns for more. Fascinated by the newly-created humans, she leaves home to see it all for herself, the farms, the cities, and the temples. Little does she know that a sex-crazed God has been lusting after her for decades. He intends her for Himself, and His obsession will change the course of her life for millennia.

In modern New York City, Chloe finally embraces her true self: After years of repressing it, she's willing to admit her own bisexual nature. Her religiously-conservative husband, however, is not, and Chloe flees the abuse that quickly follows. What she doesn't know is that a creature from legend, a myth come to life – Medusa herself – has been hiding in plain sight, and they are about to come face-to-face.

One woman's deity cursed her for being true to herself. The other woman's deity won't allow her to become her true self. Together, they might have the strength to overcome, and to embrace the divine.

(LGBTQ Romance/Mythological Fantasy for adults)

"Medusa: Dawn of a Goddess"
In the ancient past, Medusa must guard her children while struggling to balance the affections of the Olympian Hephaestus, the God of the forge.

In modern New York City, Chloe is thrilled to finally be in a healthy relationship - even if it's with a woman born from the dawn of time. Her estranged husband, however, is working with a hunter to slay the "demon" who led her astray - though he has no idea the hunt is being led by the Goddess Athena.

(LGBTQ Romance/Mythological Fantasy for adults)
(Forthcoming, TBA)

"The Initiate: The Tales of Zhava Book 1"

Zhava's life was planned for her: She was promised in marriage to a respectable trader's son across the mountains. But as her father negotiated the bride-price, the King's guards showed up, paid him more than he asked, and took her away. As one blessed by the Gods, Zhava can control the wind and small rocks - and most impressive of all, fire. Now an Initiate at the King's training center, Zhava must study the kingdom's holy book, learn to fight with a sword, and hardest of all, take firm control of her Gods-given Abilities.

Not all is safe for her and the other trainees, however. Students and even soldiers are vanishing in the night, stolen away by a mighty creature out of legend. Worst of all, the creature is controlled by a shadowy figure who quotes an evil God and seems determined to kill anyone loyal to the King - especially those blessed with Abilities such as Zhava's.

7,000 years ago, when the Gods bestowed their gifts, one girl received more than she ever dreamed.

(Fantasy for young adults)

"The Novice: The Tales of Zhava Book 2"

Zhava is doing well in her new life: she has many friends, she's learning to use her magical abilities, and she's been promoted to Novice rank. But when everything seems to be going her way, tragedy strikes: her parents are kidnapped and sold into slavery – and her former fiancé is behind it. Transferred to the command of the King's guard, Zhava and her friends must retake the farmstead and rescue her family.

But the kidnapping is not that simple. High Priest Viekoosh, follower of an evil God, is manipulating things behind the scenes. He's gathering an army of cult followers in the desert to start a war between the kingdoms, and he's employed a pair of mercenaries to capture Zhava: a woman who wields water with as much force as Zhava controls fire, and a powerful giant almost impervious to magic.

With time running out to rescue her parents, and her friends in danger from mercenary thugs, Zhava must learn to balance sword with fire, security with danger...and her mission to rescue her family against the lives of her friends.

(Fantasy for young adults)

"The Apprentice: The Tales of Zhava Book 3"

The evil Salient Kretsch escapes his confines in the King's dungeon, and Zhava is blamed. Can she catch the fugitive and clear her name?

(Fantasy for young adults)

(forthcoming, TBA)

"A Revelation of Our Savior, with Translation and Commentary by Dr. Michel S. Curllen"
Award-Winning Finalist in Religious Fiction at the 2021 American Fiction Awards*

Hidden in the forests of Romania, buried deep underground, a treasure house of secret documents has been kept out of sight for millennia.

When a team of researchers accidentally discovers the documents, warnings are whispered. People vanish. The camp suffers a midnight attack. And a secret order of religious zealots will stop at nothing to keep the truth from being revealed to the world. But what is that truth?

Dr. Michel S. Curllen is the only person to survive the tragedy and escape with the secret documents. Now, in his own words, he describes the harrowing account of the most significant discovery of ancient artifacts to happen in over 75 years – and you can read one of those documents for yourself: The Revelation of Simon, a follower of the Christ. Painstakingly translated by Dr. Curllen, including an in-depth analysis of the Revelation, you can decide for yourself what it was that was so dangerous that people had to die, and Dr. Curllen had to suffer so much.

Hidden for 2,000 years. Protected by a secret order. Read what was never meant to be seen again.

(Religious Fiction for adults)

"The Jungle God"
Winner in Science Fiction at the 2001 South West Writers*

Riches beyond their wildest imaginations – all they have to do is collect the gems...on an alien planet; deep within a jungle from which no one has ever returned; and guarded by supernatural forces no human was meant to see.

Three teams are vying to reach the gems first: Jake's devoted years of his life to finding the gems and gaining untold wealth. Rhaina, his ex-girlfriend, has a team that's fully-funded by a businessman who happens to be inconveniently dead. Tone is a member of an eco-terrorism organization barely holding together inside a dilapidated lunar base, and he knows that much money could fund their organization for millennia.

However, the Lygmies, the planet's indigenous population, have other plans. They know far more than they're willing to reveal, the jungle's wild animals are unnervingly sentient – and they obey the Lygmies' commands. Now a race to steal gems might be a race for survival – not just for Jake, Rhaina, and Tone, but for the entire human population on this violent planet. Because the Lygmies demand freedom from their human invaders, and they're willing to resurrect the most violent God in their ancient history to achieve it.

What can stop a creature so powerful, so bloodthirsty, and so chaotic He's willing to destroy everything in His path just because it's fun?

(Science Fiction for adults)

"The Redemption of Bes"

12-year-old Khoury wants to enjoy her Christmas vacation, but her best friend Isabella has other plans: Together, they accidentally resurrect an ancient Egyptian God. Bes is a household God from over 3,000 years ago who was responsible for protecting mothers and children - but he did something terribly wrong, and now He's in danger of being devoured by the crocodile Goddess Ammit.

Khoury and her friends have three days to help Bes become a better person...er, a better God...before He faces judgment. The problem? He's given up any hope of being redeemed, and He only wants to have a good time and party, even if it means getting everyone else into trouble.

With the Goddess of justice, Ma'at, counting down the days to judgment, can Khoury persuade Bes to do better?

(Fantasy for upper-grade school children)

(forthcoming, Fall 2022)

CPSIA information can be obtained
at www.ICGtesting.com
Printed in the USA
LVHW020720230523
747705LV00002B/12